YELLOWSTONE

*A Camper's Guide to the World's
First National Park*

PAUL SPERL

21st Century Campers

ISBNs:
979-8-9855147-0-4 (Ebook)
979-8-9855147-1-1 (Print)

Publisher:
21st Century Campers

CONTENTS

WHY A GUIDE TO YELLOWSTONE?

We visited Yellowstone National Park when our three kids were young, and had a blast. The geysers, mud pots, colorful hot springs, and steaming fumaroles gave the place a look that no amusement park could match, and the variety of wildlife from bison to bighorn sheep, moose, and elk filled us all with wonder. We had a wonderful time camping in a 24-foot travel trailer in Fishing Bridge RV Park.

Over the years, we've camped a lot with our kids, visiting a number of national parks as they grew up. As they got into high school and then college, other activities started to take precedence and we gradually camped less and less until we finally decided to sell the camper. Now that the kids have grown, we've purchased a 25-foot motorhome and have begun camping again, just the two of us. Our first major trip in the motorhome was to Yellowstone, and as we did our research, we were surprised at how difficult it was to find information on campgrounds in and around the park. We spent a lot of time researching in books (which were more geared toward hotel travel) and on the web prior to that trip and decided that a guide geared toward people staying in Yellowstone's campgrounds would be helpful. This book is the result of that realization.

We've visited the park several times now and have stayed at most of its campgrounds. We've outfitted our RV with solar panels so we can enjoy the comforts of home without the need for hookups or a gas generator. Much of the information in this book comes from personal experience. Although there are a number of hotels and lodges within the park, we can't imagine staying in Yellowstone without the experience camping affords. How can you enjoy a place like Yellowstone without cooking dinner outside around a campfire, seeing deer walk by your site, or sitting outside to enjoy the stars appear in the dark night sky?

This book was written from the perspective of campers to highlight the features of each of Yellowstone's twelve drive-in campgrounds. Campground descriptions include reasons for selecting a particular facility along with a list of the amenities there, including the nearest showers, emergency services, groceries, and other essentials. Nearby activities and hikes are also enumerated. In addition, we've provided a list and descriptions of both public and private campgrounds located outside the park, which can be handy in the event you can't find a site inside.

ABOUT 21ˢᵗ CENTURY CAMPERS

We are here to help you enjoy the outdoors with information on where to go, how to camp, and what to buy to make your experience the most enjoyable. We've been camping for over 50 years in tents, travel trailers, and motorhomes. We want to share our experience to make yours more comfortable and enjoyable. Whether it's planning a trip to a national park, upgrading your RV, or buying your first rig, we can help.

We love camping in our national parks and other scenic areas. We also like to be comfortable while we're there, which is why we chose a smaller motorhome that fits in most national park campgrounds and outfitted it so we can spend up to a week camping without needing any hookups.

Old Faithful Geyser erupts at about 90-minute intervals.

OVERVIEW OF YELLOWSTONE

Imagine the largest lake above 7000 feet in North America, pristine rivers, world-class waterfalls, canyons, and mountains. Add a variety of wildlife, including bison, pronghorn antelope, wolves, black and grizzly bears, moose, deer, and bighorn sheep, and you've got the makings of a great national park. Yellowstone does the typical mountain park site one better by adding a layer of unbelievably stunning geothermal features. From the eruptions of Old Faithful to the colors of the Morning Glory Pool and Grand Prismatic Spring to the bubbling Artist's Paint Pots and Mammoth's Terraces, there seems to be another treat around every corner. Oh, and it has a colorful canyon with two waterfalls at its head—worthy of a national park all its own.

Native Americans knew of the wonders of Yellowstone for centuries, but no European had visited the area until after Lewis and Clark's Corps of Discovery expedition in 1804 through1806. They managed to miss Yellowstone, but John Colter, a member of the Corps, is generally accepted as the first white man to have explored parts of what is now Yellowstone National Park during his travels from 1807 to 1810 in search of beaver pelts for the hat trade. Another mountain man and trapper, Jim Bridger, visited the area in the 1840s and returned with unbelievable stories of columns of water spouting into the air. These reports led to more expeditions into the Yellowstone area in the 1860s and early 1870s. Reports of this strange and wonderful landscape led Congress and President Grant to approve a bill that set aside "a certain tract of land lying near the headwaters of the Yellowstone River" as the world's first national park in 1872.

Over the 150 years since the park was founded, it has undergone a number of changes. Initially there was little funding and no park service to maintain it. In the 1890s, the US Army took control of the park and brought some order to the chaos, building a fort at Mammoth Hot Springs for its officers and men. The National Park service took over the park from the army when it was founded in 1916 and has run it since then. At first, the focus of the Park Service was on preserving scenery; wildlife was viewed as either a side entertainment (in the case of bears) or as a nuisance to be eliminated (wolves). That has evolved over the past 50 years or so as programs to eliminate human feeding of the bears and other animals were introduced and wolves have been brought back into the park to take their place in its ecosystem.

The Basics

Yellowstone National Park lies largely within the state of Wyoming, with parts extending into Montana and Idaho. It covers over 3000 square miles—about the size of the state of Delaware—and sees over four million visitors from around the world each year. The park has five entrances and a figure-eight roadway allowing for navigation from one point to another. The speed limit in the park is 45 mph, and you can expect delays due to road conditions, construction, and animals in or near the roadway, so make sure to allow plenty of time to get from Point A to Point B.

The northern part of the park includes attractions such as Mammoth Hot Springs, Tower Fall, the Absaroka Mountains, and the Lamar Valley. Toward the park's center, you'll find the Grand Canyon of the Yellowstone, Norris Geyser Basin, and Mount Washburn; the southern part of the park is home to Yellowstone Lake, Upper Geyser Basin (home of the Old Faithful geyser), and Midway Geyser Basin.

How to Use This Guide

We've developed this guide to help people get the most out of their visit when they are planning to camp in any of the park's twelve developed campgrounds. We start with Mammoth Campground by the North Entrance and move clockwise to the campgrounds around the park. For each campground, we include a description, map, list of amenities, and locations of the nearest services. After these basics, we list some of the main attractions in the vicinity of each campground. We have also included information on the many National Forest Service campgrounds outside the park as well as the closest campgrounds in the nearby Grand Teton National Park and private campgrounds in the gateway towns of West Yellowstone and Gardiner.

Please note that the information in this guide was as accurate as possible at the time it was written, but conditions in the park are constantly changing due to weather, geologic activity, construction, and wildlife, among other things. Most recently, COVID-19 has impacted the park as restrictions limit the number of international workers who staff the campgrounds, hotels, restaurants, etc. Some have had shortened seasons and some have adjusted their services while others have not opened for the season at all. Check the internet, visitor centers, or at the park entrance for the latest information on closures and other changes.

Map of Yellowstone

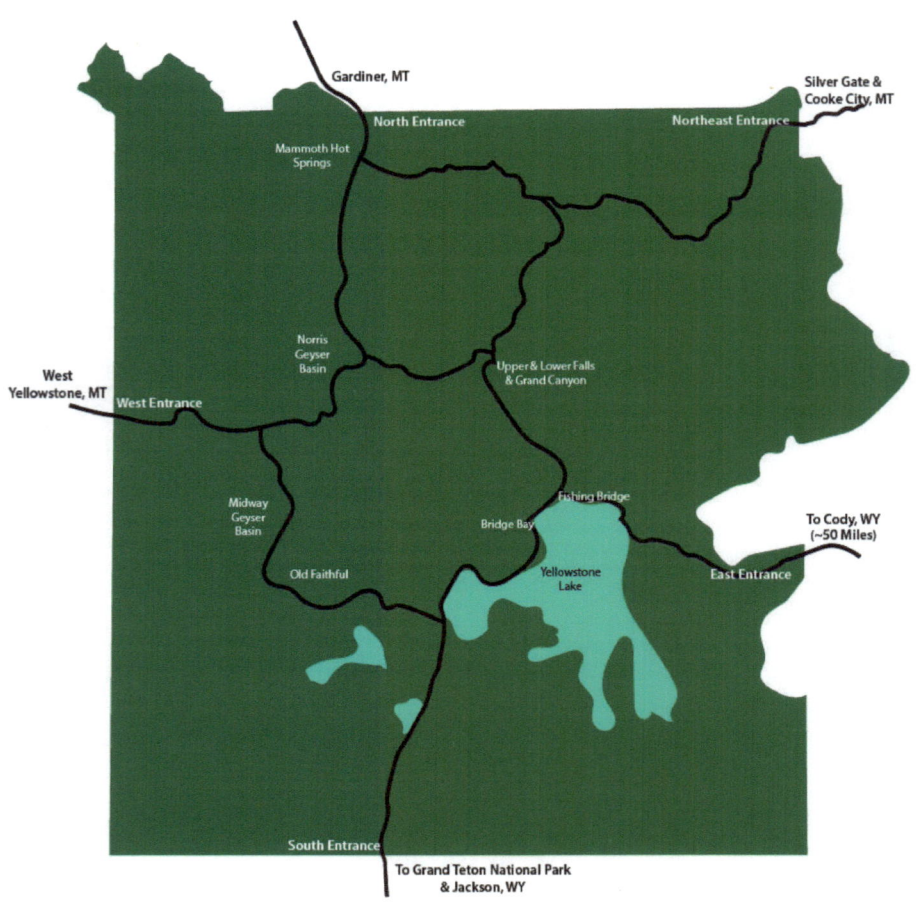

Overview of the Yellowstone Area

Weather

The campgrounds at Yellowstone are at 6200 to 7900 feet above sea level, and even in August temperatures can drop below freezing at night. At these altitudes spring comes late, and summers are short. Many of the mountain passes do not open until May and close by mid-October due to snow. Be prepared for cool weather with layered clothing regardless of when you visit.

Busy Season

July and August are the busiest months of the year in Yellowstone. June and September have historically been less crowded, although in recent years, more retired baby boomers have realized the advantages of the smaller crowds in these "shoulder" months. Restaurants, stores, and campgrounds also start to close for the season after Labor Day as the park get less crowded.

Staying Connected in Yellowstone

Before you leave for the park, download the NPS Yellowstone app to your phone, available for free on iOS and Android. The app offers live updates on campground fill times, geyser eruptions, and other information, but be aware that cell service is spotty at best and the only place in the park that offers free Wi-Fi is the Albright Visitor Center in Mammoth Hot Springs. (Wi-Fi is available to registered guests at some park lodges.) Verizon seems to have the best coverage, followed by AT&T. Other carriers are less robust. It's a good idea to check with your provider before you leave home. Service is available in most of the communities near the park and along the main highways. Due to the spotty coverage in the park, we strongly recommend that you download anything you might need before you leave home using the "Download Offline Content" option in the app's settings menu, which will load maps and other content to your phone's hard drive.

Emergency Services

The service station at Fishing Bridge offers fuel as well as RV and auto repairs.

In an emergency, dial 911 if you have phone service. Medical services are available at Mammoth Clinic (307-344-7965) in Mammoth Hot Springs year-round. In the summer there are medical services available at Lake Clinic (307-242-7241) and Old Faithful Clinic (307-545-7325) in the Lake and Old Faithful Villages, respectively. These clinics can handle injuries and illnesses, perform x-rays, conduct some tests, and offer pharmaceutical services. For cases requiring more complex services, they can arrange transport to hospitals outside the park.

Gasoline and diesel fuel are available at six locations in the park, all of which allow 24/7 fueling with a credit card. Four of these locations also offer wrecker service and repairs. You can call (406) 848-7548 if you need assistance.

Service Stations in Yellowstone				
Service Station	*24hr Fuel*	*Wrecker*	*Repairs*	*LP Gas*
Canyon	Y	Y	Y	Y
Fishing Bridge	Y	Y	Y	Y
Mammoth Hot Springs	Y	N	N	Y
Old Faithful	Y	Y	Y	Y
Tower-Roosevelt	Y	N	N	N
Grant	Y	Y	Y	Y

Two RV repair companies are authorized to provide services in the park: Mobile RV Tech (406-682-4100) and Motorcoach Maintenance and Truck Repair (406-388-7448).

Safety in Yellowstone

Yellowstone has some unique safety concerns that everyone should be aware of including its altitude, thermal features and its ever-present wildlife.

Hiking Safety

Before heading out on any hike, make sure you have enough water for everyone in your group. Bring extra, because elevation, heat, and wind in the mountains can lead to dehydration. Don't expect to drink from lakes or streams without treating or filtering the water to remove dangerous bacteria. Always carry a first aid kit, map, and a compass or GPS—and know how to use them. A flashlight and sunscreen are also recommended, as are insect repellent and bear spray.

Altitude

Much of Yellowstone is above 7000 feet in elevation. For most of us who live at lower elevations, it can take a while to adjust to the lower oxygen levels in the air. For the first few days in the park, plan less strenuous activities, limit alcohol intake, and be sure to drink plenty of water as your body acclimates.

Thermal Features

They're called thermal features for a reason—they are hot! The geysers, mud pots, hot springs, and fumaroles are all fed by super-heated underground water. That's easy to see with the steam and spray from a geyser, but even the placid-looking hot springs are extremely hot—over 190 °F (88 °C). Don't dip your finger (or toe) in—you'll likely get scalded. Also, be careful when walking near thermal features as the crust may be thin and break, causing burns or even death.

Wildlife

Yellowstone has an amazing array of wildlife, but it's up to you to keep yourself and the animals safe by following these park rules:

- Stay at least 100 yards (91m) from bears and wolves and a minimum of 25 yards (23m) from all other animals.
- If an animal moves closer to you, you need to move away to maintain the proper distance. Remember, the park is *their* home, and you're a visitor in it.
- Do not surround, crowd, or disrupt an animal's path of movement.
- If other visitors put you or wildlife in danger, report them to a park ranger.
- Spotlighting (viewing animals with artificial light) is illegal.
- Calling to attract wildlife is illegal. You may not bugle to elk, howl to wolves, or make bird calls of any kind.
- Tracking wildlife with electronic equipment is not permitted.

In addition to the above rules, it is also important to store food properly and never to feed any animals. Campsites have bear boxes for food storage—inside a hard-sided camper or vehicle works too. Keep all food, trash, and any scented items inside bear boxes or other bear-proof containers. Do not leave water or beverage containers, cooking or eating utensils, stoves, grills, coolers, garbage (bagged or not), any food (even in a container), cosmetics, or pails, buckets, and washbasins unattended at any time.

Bear Safety

Yellowstone is a bear habitat, and any time you're hiking in bear country, you may encounter one. It's important that you keep the following in mind:

- Be alert. Watch for bears, bear tracks, and scat.

- Make noise. Sing, shout, or clap your hands. Note that experts say bear bells do not work.
- Carry bear spray, and know how to use it.
- Do not hike alone. Groups of three or more are less likely to have problems with bears.
- If you encounter a bear, do not run: back away slowly.

Bear spray is available for sale at many stores in the park and for rent at a kiosk in the north end of the Canyon Visitor Center parking lot. Bear spray does have a shelf life and cannot be taken on airplanes or thrown in the trash. Canisters can be recycled at ranger stations, general stores, backcountry offices, and hotel front desks in the park.

Bison Safety

Every year there seems to be a story in the news about someone who was injured because they got too close to a bison. These majestic beasts look and act like cattle much of the time, but you need to remember that they are wild animals and maintain that 25-yard distance from them. If they're on or near a trail, go around them – off trail if necessary – to maintain your separation. And please: never, ever have your wife/child/brother-in-law

They may look docile, but remember, bison are bigger, stronger, faster, and probably meaner than you are.

or anyone else pose for a picture with the nice bison, or worse yet, try to take a selfie with one.

The Best of Yellowstone

Upper Geyser Basin (Old Faithful Geyser)

Containing the most recognizable feature of the park—the Old Faithful Geyser—the Upper Geyser Basin is *the* don't-miss area in Yellowstone. Plan on a minimum of half a day to a day to explore the area and the adjacent Black Sand and Biscuit basins. Nearest campgrounds: Grant and Madison.

The Grand Canyon of the Yellowstone

Headed by two impressive waterfalls, the Grand Canyon of the Yellowstone is 1000 feet deep and 20 miles long. Roads parallel both its north and south rims, offering multiple opportunities to both explore along the rim and venture into the canyon for a better look. Allow at least a half day to a day to take in the canyon. Nearest campground: Canyon.

Mammoth Hot Springs Terraces

You can almost see the minerals forming on top of the water like ice on a winter puddle. Wander the boardwalks and take in the ever-changing beauty of the travertine terraces. Nearest campground: Mammoth.

Norris Geyser Basin

This is actually two geyser basins, Porcelain and Back Basin, and includes the largest geyser in the world: Steamboat Geyser. It doesn't erupt often, but when it does, it can send water over 300 feet in the air. Nearest campgrounds: Norris and Mammoth.

Lamar Valley

This is the place to be if you want to view wildlife. Bison, bears, wolves, and pronghorn antelope are among the animals to be viewed in the valley. Nearest campgrounds: Slough Creek, Pebble Creek, and Tower Fall.

Midway Geyser Basin

Contains the world's third-largest hot spring, Grand Prismatic Spring, a stunning display of shimmering turquoise water surrounded by orange and brown whorls of thermophiles – bacteria that thrives in the hot runoff from the spring. Don't miss the aerial view of the spring, which you can access from the Fairy Falls Trail. Nearest campground: Madison.

Hayden Valley

Another great spot to view wildlife along the Yellowstone River as it makes its way from Fishing Bridge to the Upper Falls. Bison and other animals are frequently seen along the river. Nearest campgrounds: Canyon and Fishing Bridge.

Lower Geyser Basin

Home to the Fountain Paint Pots, a collection of mud pots as well as a number of geysers, hot springs, and fumaroles including the Great Fountain Geyser, which can shoot water over 200 feet in the air every 10-14 hours. Nearest campground: Madison.

Yellowstone Lake

The largest lake above 7000 feet in the US, Yellowstone Lake offers a variety of water activities from paddling to powerboating as well as tours of the lake. Nearest campgrounds: Fishing Bridge, Bridge Bay and Grant.

Getting into the Park

The Roosevelt Arch welcomes visitors to the North Entrance to the park.

There are five entrances to the park: the North Entrance in Gardiner, MT; Northeast Entrance near Cooke City–Silver Gate, MT; East Entrance 50 miles west of Cody, WY; South Entrance near Grand Teton National Park; and the West Entrance outside West Yellowstone, MT.

North Entrance

Follow US Highway 89 south from I-90 in Livingston along the Yellowstone River through Yankee Jim Canyon to the North Entrance of Yellowstone National Park in Gardiner, Montana. Gardiner is the second-largest gateway community to Yellowstone and has a wide variety of amenities including shops, restaurants, lodging, and RV parks. The original entrance road goes through the Roosevelt Arch just south of Gardiner. Passenger cars can enter through the arch, but RVs and trailers should follow the signs and take the shortcut from Park Street. After going through the entrance station, it's about a five-mile drive to Mammoth Hot Springs. The North Entrance is open year-round.

Northeast Entrance

The Northeast Entrance to the park is west of Cooke City–Silver Gate, Montana, on US Highway 212. It's accessed from either Red Lodge, Montana, via the Beartooth Highway (see Appendix A for more information) or Cody, Wyoming, via the Chief Joseph Highway, both of which offer stunning views as you enter the

Absaroka Mountains. Highway 212 closes from mid-October to late May each year due to snow in the higher elevations. It's about 10 miles from the gate to Pebble Creek campground and 30 miles to the Tower–Roosevelt area.

East Entrance

About 50 miles west of Cody, Wyoming, on US Highway 14/16/20 is the East Entrance to Yellowstone National Park. The highway is a scenic drive along the banks of the North Fork of the Shoshone River in Shoshone National Forest with several National Forest Service campgrounds along the way. It is about 27 miles from the East Entrance to the Fishing Bridge/Lake Yellowstone area.

South Entrance

The South Entrance to Yellowstone lies on US Highway 89/191/287 just north of Grand Teton National Park. About 12 miles north of this entrance is Lewis Lake campground. The park hub of West Thumb is 22 miles north of the South Entrance.

West Entrance

The largest city adjacent to the park is West Yellowstone, which contains the West Entrance to the park. West Yellowstone has a wide variety of tourist amenities, including hotels, full-hookup campgrounds, restaurants, grocery stores, and gift shops. It's the closest entrance to the geysers (including Old Faithful) and other thermal features in the western part of the park. Madison Campground is about 14 miles from the West Entrance, and Old Faithful Village is about 30 miles away.

Admission and Fees

A pass is required to enter the park; there are several options to choose from.

Yellowstone Seven-Day Passes

Good for entry into Yellowstone National Park for seven days from the date of purchase. Purchase at the entrance station or get a digital version at https://www.recreation.gov/sitepass/72451/.

Private, noncommercial vehicle: $35

Motorcycle or snowmobile: $30

Individual (by foot, bicycle, ski, etc.): $20/person

Yellowstone Annual Pass

Provides free entrance into Yellowstone National Park for one year (valid through the month of purchase). Can be purchased at the gate or at https://www.recreation.gov/sitepass/72451/.

Yellowstone National Park Annual Pass: $70

America the Beautiful—The National Parks and Recreation Lands Annual Pass

Covers entrance fees at all national parks and national wildlife refuges as well as day-use fees at national forests and grasslands and at lands managed by the Bureau of Land Management, Bureau of Reclamation, and US Army Corps of Engineers. This pass covers the fees listed above for a driver and all passengers in a personal vehicle at per-vehicle fee areas or up to four adults at sites that charge per person.

The passes can be purchased in person at a federal recreation site, online at the USGS store (https://store.usgs.gov/pass/), or by phone at (888) ASK-USGS (1-888-275-8747), extension 3 (8 a.m. to 4 p.m. Mountain Time)
Entry into national parks and recreation lands for one year from purchase: $80

Senior Pass

Available for US citizens or permanent residents age 62 or over. Applicants must provide documentation of age and residency or citizenship.

Purchase in person at a federal recreation site, online at the USGS store (https://store.usgs.gov/senior-pass/) or through the mail using this application form: https://store.usgs.gov/s3fs-public/senior_pass_application.pdf/. There is an additional cost of $10 for passes purchased online or by mail.

The Senior Pass may also provide a 50 percent discount on some amenity fees charged for facilities and services such as camping, swimming, boat launch, and specialized interpretive services. The Senior Pass generally does NOT cover or reduce special recreation permit fees or fees charged by concessioners.

Lifetime Senior Pass: $80

Annual Senior Pass: $20

Free Annual Pass for US Military

Available to current US military members and dependents in the Army, Navy, Air Force, Marines, and Coast Guard as well as Reserve and National Guard members. You can obtain the card at any federal recreation site by showing a Common Access Card (CAC) or Military ID (Form 1173).

All passes are nontransferable. For more information on annual passes, go to https://www.nps.gov/planyourvisit/passes.htm/.

Driving in Yellowstone

The main roads in Yellowstone are paved and generally in good shape. There's a short window in the summer when road construction is possible, so in most years, some section of road in the park will be under construction. Check the road conditions online at https://www.nps.gov/yell/planyourvisit/road-construction.htm/ or at visitor centers and entrance stations, and plan accordingly. The speed limit is 45 miles per hour in the park unless posted lower. Many of the roads have little or no shoulder and can be a bit challenging for wider vehicles such as motorhomes or travel trailers. There are a number of mountain passes in and around the park, and larger vehicles should take care to downshift on descents to avoid overheating brakes.

Parking at the more popular attractions can be a challenge for cars, let alone recreational vehicles. To make sure you get a spot, it's a good idea to try to get to your destination by 9:00 a.m. before the crowds really build up, especially if you're driving your RV.

YELLOWSTONE'S CAMPGROUNDS

Campground Overview

Yellowstone has a dozen campgrounds within the park ranging in size from as few as 16 campsites to several with more than 400 sites. All have water (sometimes hand-pumped) and at least vault toilets. Many have restrooms with flush toilets, and several have shower facilities. Only one, Fishing Bridge RV Park, has sites with hookups (electric, water, and sewer) and it is only open to hard-sided camping units (no tents or tent campers) due to bear activity in the area. (Note—Fishing Bridge RV Park was closed for remodeling 2019-2021 and is expected to reopen in 2022.) The five largest campgrounds are operated by a private company (Yellowstone National Park Lodges); the rest are run by the National Park Service. The table below gives a brief overview of the amenities at each campground.

Campground	Season	Rate (2022)	Sites	Longest Site (Total Vehicle)	Toilets	Showers	Reservations	Full Hookups	Generators Allowed	Dump Station	Details on page	Comments
Mammoth*	All Year	$ 25	85	65'	F	N	Y	N	Y	N	21	35' limit in winter.
Tower Falls*	Early Jun-Early Sep	$ 20	31	30'	V	N	Y	N	N	N	29	Tight turn on campground road.
Slough Creek*	Mid Jun-Mid Oct	$ 20	16	30'	V	N	Y	N	N	N	37	Excellent for wildlife viewing.
Pebble Creek*	Mid Jun-Late Sep	$ 20	27	45'	V	N	Y	N	N	N	40	Some long pull-throughs. Sites 1-16 reservable.
Canyon	Late May-Late Sep	$ 34	273	40'	F	Y	Y	N	Y	Y	47	Full services at Canyon village
Fishing Bridge	Late May - Early Oct	$ 83	310	95'	F	Y	Y	Y	Y	Y	64	Plan to open in 2022 after renovations
Bridge Bay	Mid May-Early Sep	$ 29	432	40'	F	Y	Y	N	Y	Y	69	Close to marina.
Grant	Early Jun-Mid Sep	$ 34	430	40'	F	Y	Y	N	Y	Y	73	On West Thumb of Yellowstone Lake.
Lewis Lake*	Mid Jun - Late Oct	$ 20	85	25'	V	N	Y	N	N	N	83	Often fills late.
Madison	Late April-Mid Oct	$ 28	278	40'	F	N	Y	N	Y	Y	87	Madison River flows by the campground.
Norris*	Mid May-Late Sep	$ 25	112	50'	F	N	Y	N	Y	N	98	Near Norris Geyser Basin
Indian Creek*	Mid Jun-Mid Sep	$ 20	70	35'	V	N	Y	N	N	N	108	Distance from road makes for quiet camping.

Campgrounds Inside Yellowstone National Park

* Operated by the National Park Service.

Interagency Access and Senior Pass holders get a 50 percent discount except at Fishing Bridge. "Longest site" refers to total combined vehicle length (trailer + tow vehicle).

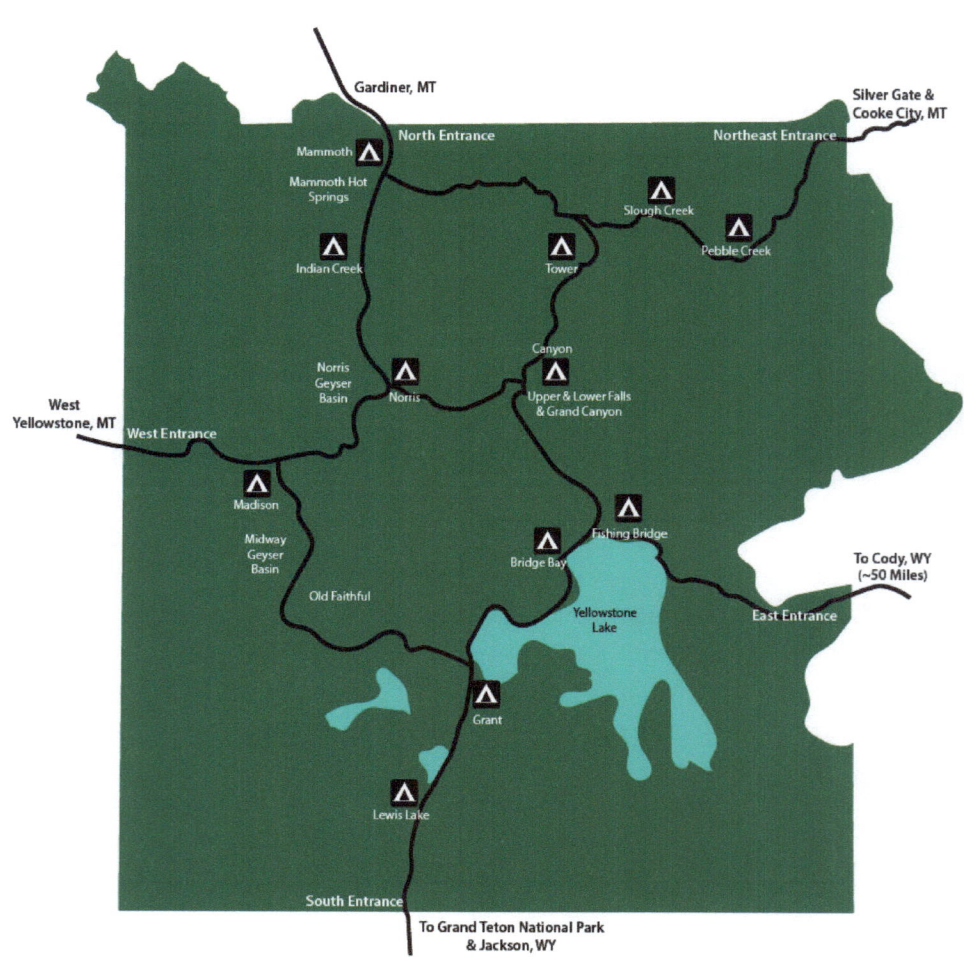

Campground locations in Yellowstone.

Reservations at the Yellowstone National Park Lodge campgrounds can be made by calling (307) 344-7311 or online at www.xanterra.com/. These campgrounds typically sell out far in advance, especially for the peak July-August season, so book early.

Reservations Policies at NPS-operated Campgrounds
Reservations policies have been evolving rapidly over the past few years. Check www.recreation.gov or https://www.nps.gov/yell/planyourvisit/campgrounds.htm for more information before planning your trip.

All of the National Park Service Campgrounds are now reservable through www.recreation.gov. Reservations at these campgrounds become available six months ahead of time and it's a good idea to book as early as possible because these sites sell out quickly. Some of the campgrounds (Indian Creek and Lewis Lake) hold back 20% of their sites until two weeks prior to arrival, so if you're unable to book at the 6-month window you still have a chance at a reservation two weeks out.

A few things to keep in mind about camping in the park:

- Reservable campgrounds book far in advance. Make reservations up to a year ahead (for Xanterra-run campgrounds; six months for NPS campgrounds) if possible.
- You are limited to no more than 14 days of camping in Yellowstone between July 1 and Labor Day and 30 days the rest of the year. This restriction does not apply to Fishing Bridge RV Park.
- No more than six people are allowed on a site.
- Overnight camping or parking is only allowed in designated campgrounds or campsites.
- Generators, where allowed, are subject to an allowable noise level of 60dB and may only be used between the hours of 8:00 a.m. and 8:00 p.m.

- Campfires (including portable firepits—gas or wood) are not allowed in Fishing Bridge RV Park. Wood or charcoal fires are allowed in all other campgrounds unless there are restrictions due to forest fire danger. Propane grills and stoves are generally not affected by forest fire restrictions.
- Fishing Bridge is the only campground offering full hook-ups within the park.
  Check the web for more information. - www.xanterra.com/
- Senior pass discounts are available at all campgrounds except Fishing Bridge.
- There are group sites available at Bridge Bay, Grant Village, and Madison campgrounds. Check https://www.nps.gov/yell/planyourvisit/campgrounds.htm/ for more information.

Camping in Yellowstone

All of the campgrounds in the park have one thing you can't get anywhere else—they're *in* Yellowstone. You can't beat the location. That said, when it comes to the actual campsites, they range from marginal to fabulous, and you don't have much control over which specific site you get. We've had sites that were just wide spots in the road with no real parking pad – in some cases with a neighbor a few feet from our bumper. The views and access to some of the most spectacular scenery and wildlife in the world more than make up for a less than perfect campsite. And some of the sites are *gorgeous*. We've had some that were so secluded that we felt like the only people in the park as we enjoyed our campfire. The main thing is to be prepared for whatever you might get when it comes to campsites. You may have to drive in instead of back in to fit in a site or make other accommodations, but most importantly, you will be inside the park.

There is no overflow camping within the park, and there is no overnight camping or vehicle parking in picnic areas, parking areas, pullouts, or any area not designated as a campground. There are a number of public and private campgrounds in the vicinity of the park. See page 82 for more information on campgrounds outside the park.

Mammoth Campground

Mammoth Campground

We have really enjoyed our stays at Mammoth Campground. It's a different experience from most of the other Yellowstone campgrounds because it's in sagebrush country rather than forested. It's a short (but steep) hike from the campground to Mammoth Hot Spring and the Fort Yellowstone historical sites, restaurants, stores, and visitor center. It has some huge (65-foot-long) pull-through sites. There are restrooms with flush toilets and water but no showers. (Pay showers are available at the Mammoth Hot Springs Hotel.) The campground is the only one in Yellowstone that's open all year, but note that there is a hairpin curve that must be negotiated that limits total vehicle length to 30'—difficult especially in winter. North Entrance Road goes rather close to the campground, which may bother some people, but we've enjoyed the hiking in the area as well as the proximity to the amenities available in Mammoth. Generators are allowed between 8 a.m. and 8 p.m., and campground hosts are available if you need help. Mammoth is now reservable for May 1 through October 15 up to six months in advance at www.recreation.gov/. The rest of the year it is first-come, first-served.

Mammoth Campground has some long pull-through sites.

Campground Details

Sites	Reservations	Elevation	Accessible Sites	Flush Toilets	Generators (60dB limit)	Big Rig?	Dump Station
85	Yes (5/1-10/15)	6800'	Yes	Yes	8 a.m.-8 p.m.	Up to 70'	No

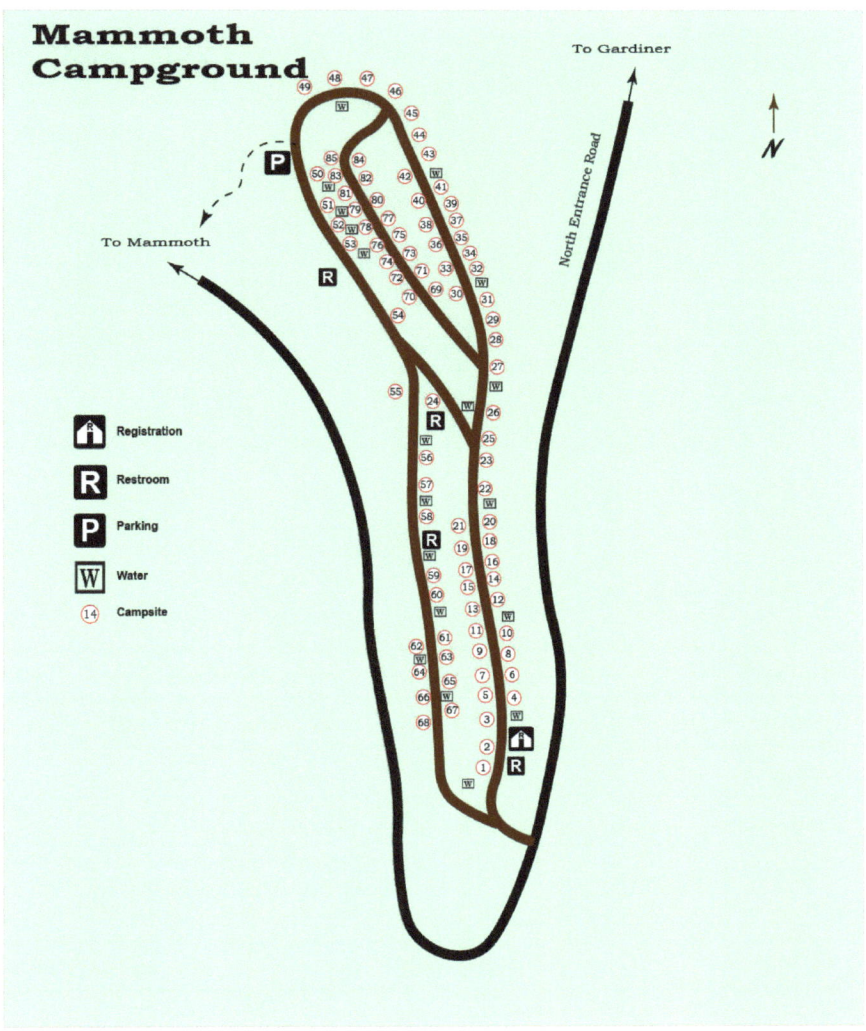

Mammoth Campground

The terraces at Mammoth Hot Springs are within walking distance of Mammoth Campground.

Nearby Amenities

Showers	Mammoth Hot Springs Hotel ($)
Dump Station	Madison or Canyon Campground
Laundry	Gardiner
Restaurant	Mammoth Village
Groceries	Gardiner
Gas	Mammoth Village
ATM	Mammoth Village
Emergency Services	Mammoth Clinic (Mammoth Village)

Nearby Activities

Mammoth Village

There's a fairly short, steep path from Mammoth Campground up to North Entrance Road that starts near the campground amphitheater, providing access to the Albright Visitor Center, Historic Fort Yellowstone, and the Mammoth Hot Springs Terraces.

Mammoth Village and Fort Yellowstone

Boardwalks and stairs enable you to observe these ever-changing thermal features up close.

Self-guided tours of Fort Yellowstone start at the Albright Visitor Center and include the parade grounds across from the visitor center, Captain's quarters, and Officer's quarters, most of which are closed since they are now occupied by park service staff or are used as offices or storage. You can also see the blacksmith shop, granary, stables, hospital, and chapel.

Mammoth Hot Springs Terraces

Southwest of the visitor center on Grand Loop Road is the entrance to a boardwalk you can take to see the 37-foot-tall Liberty Cap, a now-dormant hot spring cone. Follow the boardwalk to Opal Spring, Palette Spring, Minerva Terrace, and Jupiter Terrace. Pick up a trail guide ($1

New rock is formed almost before your eyes as the hot water cools and minerals solidify.

donation) and follow the boardwalks to see these ever-changing thermal features. Be aware that the boardwalk has a lot of stairs, which can make the walking strenuous.

Trails

Beaver Ponds Loop Trail

Starting between the Liberty Cap and the stone house, the Beaver Ponds Trail climbs for about a mile before flattening out into more rolling terrain, passing an old beaver pond and dam. You'll pass through Douglas fir forests, aspen groves, and sagebrush before descending to Old Gardiner Road behind the Mammoth Hotel. It's a moderately strenuous hike about 5½ miles long, ending near the campground.

The first part of the Beaver Ponds hike is through forest …

Boiling River Trail

OK, it's not actually boiling, but there is a hot spring that discharges into the Gardiner River about halfway between Mammoth and Gardiner, making the river warm enough to bathe in. There are two choices to get there. You can drive to the Boiling River Trailhead (about 2.5 miles south of Gardiner) and enjoy a fairly easy and level half-mile hike to the swimming hole, or you can take the Lava

… and it ends up in open sagebrush country.

Creek Trail across from the campground on North Entrance Road and take a left at the junction with the Boiling River Trail. The second option is a bit more challenging because the trail is less developed and you'll have about a 300-foot climb to get back to the campground.

This is a very popular hike; you can expect to see dozens of people on the trail and in the water on a warm summer afternoon. There are no changing facilities, and swimsuits are required. Glass containers are not allowed and there is no swimming in the hot spring, only in the river. The area may be closed to swimming for safety in times of high spring runoff.

Tower Fall Campground

Tower Fall Campground

Close to the Tower General Store and perched on a hillside above Tower Fall, this campground has 31 sites and can handle RVs up to

Tower Campground has some nice tent campsites.

30 feet long. There is a tight turn within the campground that may be challenging for longer rigs. Sites have picnic tables and firepits with grates as well as shared food storage boxes. A hand-pumped water faucet is available along with vault toilets. Generators are not allowed. Showers are available a short drive away in Roosevelt Lodge at Tower Junction. Inquire at the front desk of the lodge for the price and location of the showers.

There's a path that starts near the top of the campground entrance road and winds down to the Tower Store where you can buy gifts, limited groceries, and supplies. There's also a small restaurant section in the store.

Deer running through Tower Fall Campground in the morning.

Campground Details

Sites	Reservations	Elevation	Accessible Sites	Flush Toilets	Generators (60dB limit)	Big Rig?	Dump Station
31	Yes	6600'	No	No (Vault)	No	Up to 30'	No

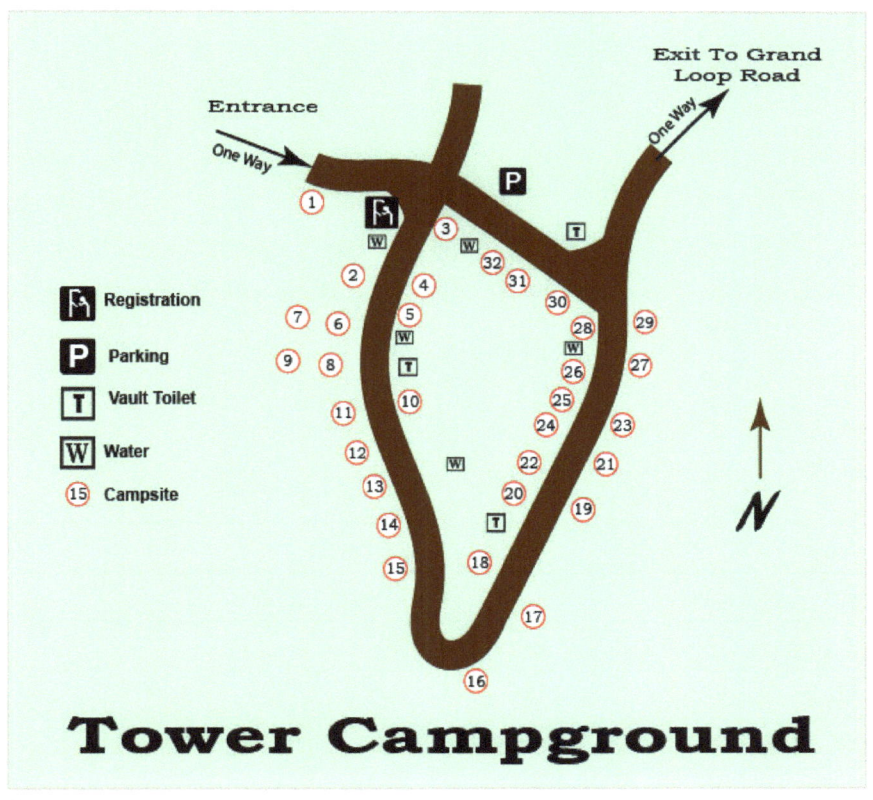

Tower Campground

Tower Fall Campground

Tower Fall is a short walk down the hill from the campground.

Nearby Amenities

Showers	Roosevelt Lodge ($)
Dump Station	Canyon Campground
Laundry	Gardiner
Restaurant	Roosevelt Lodge
Groceries	Gardiner (limited supplies at Tower Store)
Gas	Tower Junction (Roosevelt Lodge)
ATM	Mammoth Village
Emergency Services	Mammoth Clinic (Mammoth Village)

Campground Activities

There are evening talks hosted by rangers at the campground amphitheater several nights a week. Consult the bulletin board at the campground for more information.

Tower amphitheater is used for regular evening ranger talks.

Tower Junction

A couple of miles north of the Tower Campground and Store is Tower Junction, home of the historic Roosevelt Lodge with its restaurant, iconic front porch, cabins, and store. Horseback riding is available at the Roosevelt Corral, where they offer one- and two-hour rides as well as stagecoach rides and an "Old West Dinner Cookout." For more information, visit www.xanterra.com. There's also a ranger station at Tower Junction.

Roosevelt Lodge is a great place to enjoy the cooks' night off.

Lamar Valley

Northeast Entrance Road ends at Tower Junction and is the route to the Lamar Valley and its wildlife. The road crosses the Yellowstone River, Lamar River, and Soda Butte Creek on its way through sagebrush country to the mountains and the Northeast Entrance. Bears, coyotes, wolves, pronghorn, bighorn sheep, and elk are among the animals to be seen here in addition to the huge herds of bison, making this the premier wildlife-watching area in the park.

Trails

Tower Fall Trail

Across from the entrance to the campground behind the Tower Fall Store on Grand Loop Road is the short (one mile) and easy Tower

Although you can no longer hike to the bottom of Tower Fall, the hike offers spectacular views.

Fall Trail, which will bring you to the point where Tower Creek enters the Yellowstone River. Erosion has closed the trail that led to the base of the falls—note that you can't see the falls from the trail that remains. Regardless, the hike is well worth the trip because it offers excellent views of the Yellowstone River as it winds its way from the Grand Canyon to the Black Canyon of the Yellowstone.

Roosevelt Lodge/Lost Lake

It's about 2½ miles from the campground to Roosevelt Lodge on a path that parallels Grand Loop Road, with occasional views of the

Yellowstone River. The path leaves from near the top of the campground entrance road where you'll quickly come to a junction. You'll want to go right. (You can also head west [left] on the unmaintained Tower Creek Trail for a walk along the creek. You'll need to ford the creek if you choose that path, so bring suitable footwear.) After about two miles, you'll come to another junction. To

View of the Yellowstone River from the Tower Fall Trail.

the right is the route to Roosevelt Lodge; the left will take you to Lost Lake. From Lost Lake, you have the option of looping around by the lakeshore or heading east—the more direct route to the lodge. There's also a short, pleasant trail behind the lodge that leads to a viewpoint of Lost Creek Falls.

Slough Creek Campground

Slough Creek Campground

If you're looking to view wildlife in Yellowstone, Slough Creek is the place to stay. Situated at the end of a two-mile dirt road off of Northeast Entrance Road near the Lamar Valley, this campground can handle RVs up to 30 feet in length. Sites have fire rings with a grate, picnic tables, and shared food storage boxes. A few of the sites are along Slough Creek, some are in an open meadow, and others are located in the trees. The campground has a hand pump for water as well as vault toilets. Generators are not allowed at any time. This is one of the most sought-after campgrounds and is now reservable at www.recreation.gov/.

Campground Details

Sites	Reservations	Elevation	Accessible Sites	Flush Toilets	Generators (60dB limit)	Big Rig?	Dump Station
16	Yes	6250'	Yes	No (Vault)	No	Up to 30'	No

Nearby Amenities

Showers	Roosevelt Lodge ($)
Dump Station	Canyon Campground
Laundry	Gardiner
Restaurant	Roosevelt Lodge
Groceries	Gardiner
Gas	Roosevelt Lodge
ATM	Mammoth Hot Springs
Emergency Services	Mammoth Clinic

N

Buffalo
Creek

Registration

T Vault Toilet

15 Campsite

Slough Creek

Tent Sites

To Northeast
Entrance Road

Slough Creek
Campground

Slough Creek Campground

The Lamar Valley has been called America's Serengeti due to its abundance of wildlife.

Campground Activities

Wildlife viewing and fishing dominate the activities at Slough Creek. There's also a lot of open space for stargazing, so bring along your binoculars or telescope and enjoy Yellowstone's dark skies.

Nearby Activities

Lamar Valley

Because it is such a great place to view wildlife, the Lamar Valley is often referred to as "America's Serengeti." Bears, bighorn sheep, elk, bison, pronghorn antelope, coyotes, and wolves all can be seen here. Get out your binoculars, spotting scope, or zoom lens and enjoy the view.

Trails

Slough Creek Trail

The Slough Creek Trailhead is on the access road just south of the campground. This is a moderately difficult trail with just 400 feet of elevation gain in 11 miles. This is an out-and-back hike, so you can go out as far as you want before you turn around. Slough Creek is known as one of the premier cutthroat trout fishing streams in the world, and you'll likely see a few fishermen trying their luck. The trail generally follows the slow, wandering creek through open country with elk, bison, and deer to be seen grazing along the way.

The Lamar River.

Lamar River Trail

About eight miles east of the road to Slough Creek campground on Northeast Entrance Road is the Lamar River Trailhead. The Lamar River Trail is a 30+ mile out-and-back trail along the Lamar River into the backcountry. The area is frequented by bears and bison, and the trail is considered moderate in difficulty. The trail intersects with the Specimen Ridge Trail about a mile from the trailhead. Soda Butte Creek and the Lamar River are both accessible from the same trailhead; both are popular with fishermen. As with the Slough Creek Trail, you can turn around after you've hiked far enough.

Pebble Creek Campground

Pebble Creek Campground

Located about nine miles from the Northeast Entrance to the park and the towns of Silver Gate and Cooke City, Pebble Creek offer

Pebble Creek offers sites among the trees and out in the sun with views of the surrounding mountains.

campers a more remote camping experience than many other campgrounds in Yellowstone. A few sites are capable of handling fairly long RVs in pull-through sites. There is also an area reserved for tent campers. Sites have picnic tables and fireplaces with grates and have shared food storage boxes. The nearest stores, restaurants, and other services are located in Silver Gate and Cooke City. A campground host is usually there to help you. Sites 1-16 are reservable six months in advance at www. recreation.gov/.

Pebble Creek is one of our favorites due to its small size, sites with good solar capability, and gorgeous mountain views. There are also opportunities to view wildlife in the fields by the campground. The grounds are only a short drive from the Northeast Entrance and the Beartooth Highway if you're looking for a respite from the rigors of life in the park.

The meadow by the campground is frequented by bears, bison, and other wildlife.

Campground Details

Sites	Reservations	Elevation	Accessible Sites	Flush Toilets	Generators (60dB limit)	Big Rig?	Dump Station
27	Yes (Sites 1-16)	6900'	1	No (Vault)	No	Up to 45'	No

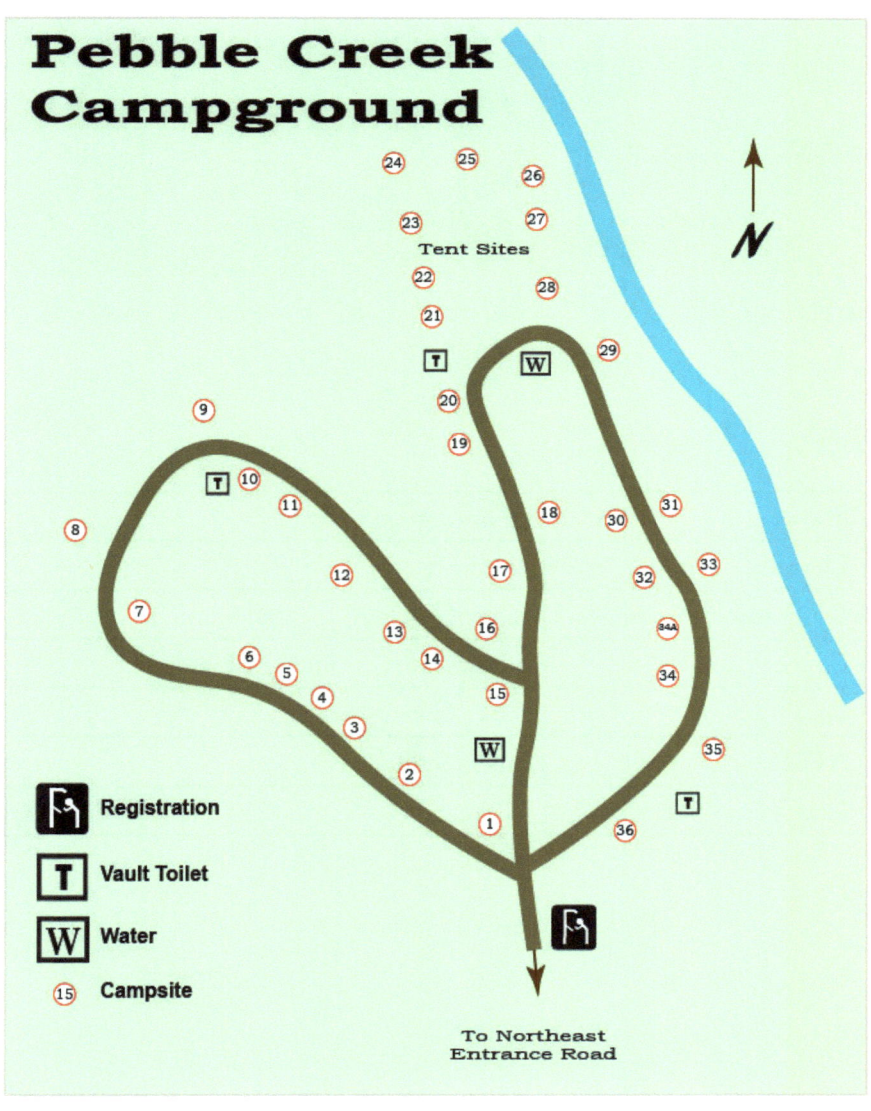

Pebble Creek Campground

The Absaroka Mountains near Pebble Creek.

Nearby Amenities

Showers	Roosevelt Lodge ($)
Laundry	Gardiner
Restaurant	Silver Gate
Groceries	Silver Gate (Limited) or Gardiner
Gas	Silver Gate
ATM	Silver Gate
Emergency Services	Mammoth

Campground Activities

Popular activities in the Pebble Creek area include fishing in Pebble Creek and Soda Butte Creek as well as wildlife viewing around both creeks and in the nearby Lamar Valley.

Several campsites at Pebble Creek are right on the water.

Nearby Activities

Hiking Trails

Pebble Creek Trail

You can pick up the trail from the campground and follow it along the creek in the Pebble Creek Valley. (The bridge across Pebble Creek was washed out in 2019, so you may need to cross the creek at the entrance road and walk along the road to the trailhead.) It's about 12 miles to the far end of the trail near the Northeast Entrance to the park, so either set up a shuttle or

A fine meadow on the Pebble Creek Trail.

turn around when you feel you've gone far enough. The trail goes through forests and meadows and moves gradually uphill after a bit of a steeper climb from the southern trailhead near the campground. It follows Pebble Creek, roughly paralleling Northeast Entrance Road, and offers some excellent views of the surrounding mountains. At the northern end, the trail drops back down to Northeast Entrance Road.

Trout Lake

The Trout Lake hike is an easy 1½-mile trek. The trailhead is 1.8 miles west of the Pebble Creek Campground on Northeast Entrance Road. There's a steep quarter-mile climb from the trailhead to the inlet of the lake, which sits in a wildflower-filled meadow. It's about a half-mile loop around the lake. Fishing is allowed in the lake (catch and release only) except at the inlet, which is closed to fishing to protect spawning trout.

Trout Lake is a pretty little lake with views of the surrounding mountains.

Canyon Campground

Canyon Campground

Its central location within the park with access to restaurants, shops, and visitor centers as well as the Grand Canyon of the Yellowstone makes Canyon Campground an attractive option. The campground accommodates RVs up to 40 feet long and has a few pull-through sites. Reservations are recommended at all times (www.yellowstonenationalpark-lodges.com), and for the July and August busy season, you'll probably need to make your reservations six months to a year in advance. There are 15 restrooms with flush toilets and cold running water in the campground as well as pay showers (two included per night) and laun-

The Camper Services building at Canyon campground has showers, firewood, and a laundry.

dry in the Camper Services building. Be aware that some campsites are more than a half-mile from the Camper Services building due to the layout of the campground. As with most Yellowstone camp-

grounds, sites may not be level, so plan accordingly. Firewood is available at the Camper Services building, and generators are allowed between 8:00 a.m. and 8:00 p.m.

Canyon Village is located about a quarter-mile from the Camper Services building and hosts the Canyon Visitor Education Center as well as the Yellowstone General Store (soda fountain/diner, gifts, outdoor supplies, books, and some groceries) and Yellowstone Adventures, a

Lack of understory on the lodgepole pines doesn't make for a lot of privacy in Canyon Campground.

specialty outdoor shop. The Canyon Lodge, also located in the village, has a cafeteria, deli, and dining room that are open for breakfast, lunch, and dinner, as well as a gift shop. In July through early September, rangers host nightly presentations on the natural and cultural history of the Yellowstone region. Check the bulletin boards for more information.

The Canyon Visitor Center is about a quarter mile from Camper Services.

Campground Details

Sites	Reservations	Elevation	Accessible Sites	Flush Toilets	Generators (60dB limit)	Big Rig?	Dump Station
273	Yes	7900'	Yes	Yes	8 a.m.–8 p.m.	Up to 40'	Yes

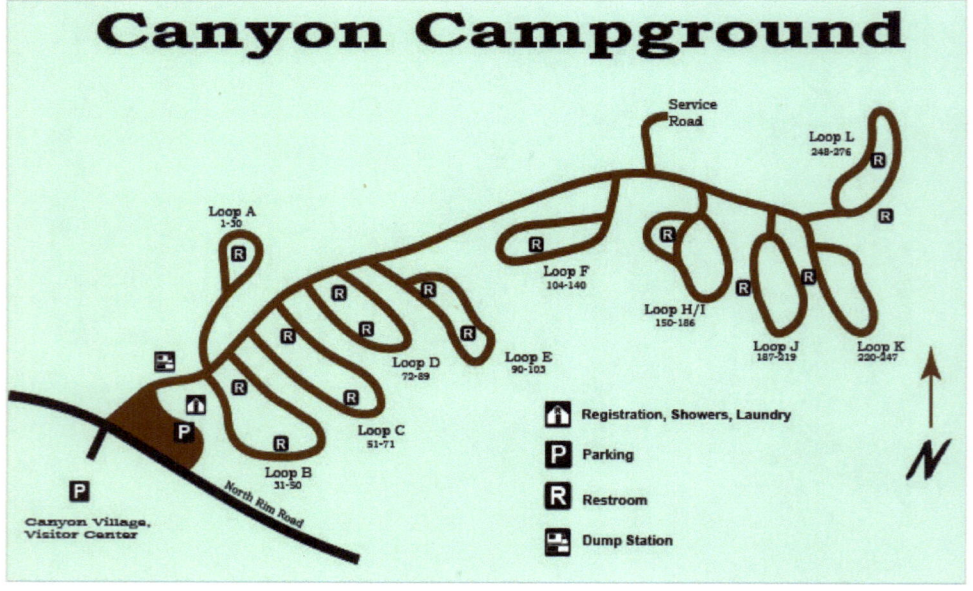

Canyon Campground

The Lower Falls of the Yellowstone.

Nearby Amenities

Showers	Canyon Campground
Laundry	Canyon Campground
Restaurant	Canyon Village
Groceries	Canyon Village
Gas	Canyon Junction
ATM	Canyon Lodge
Emergency Services	Lake Village

Nearby Attractions

Grand Canyon of the Yellowstone

Stunning views of the Grand Canyon of the Yellowstone seem to be around every corner.

At over a thousand feet deep and 20 miles long, the Grand Canyon of the Yellowstone would be worthy of its own national park if it weren't already located in Yellowstone. A pair of waterfalls mark the beginning of the canyon, with the Upper Falls dropping over 100 feet and the Lower Falls plunging another 300-plus feet into the canyon. There are trails and drives on both rims of the canyon, each with many opportunities to view the falls and canyon from various angles. Trail guides are available at visitor centers and include information on the trails, geology, and wildlife of the area.

The canyon from Grand View Overlook.

North Rim

The one-way North Rim Drive starts about a mile south of Canyon Junction on Grand Loop Road. There are accessible walkways and overlooks at multiple points along the road. The Brink of the Lower Falls Trail offers an opportunity to view the falls up close and personal after a descent of about 600 feet. It's a long walk back up, but well worth the effort.

The brink of the Lower Falls.

A half-mile or so along the rim road is the Lookout Point parking area, where you can find several paved overlooks adjacent to the lot. Follow the trail that begins at the Lookout Point signs, stay left at the fork, and you'll be treated to a full view of the Lower Falls and the canyon. Red Rock Trail gives the adventurous hiker an opportunity to descend partway (about 500 feet) into the canyon for a more striking view of the Lower Falls. This trail forks to the right from the path from the parking lot.

Grand View Overlook offers another accessible view of the canyon along North Rim Drive and the Yellowstone River. A half-mile or so further along North Rim Drive is the road to Inspiration Point. This newly reconstructed walkway offers spectacular views of the canyon.

About a half-mile south of the North Rim Drive on Grand Loop Road, you can find the short road to the Brink of

It's a lot of stairs, but the Red Rock Trail offers unique views of the falls and canyon.

the Upper Falls parking area. It's a short walk to the falls, where you can feel the power of the Yellowstone River as it begins its descent into the canyon.

The Yellowstone River begins its descent into the Grand Canyon at the Upper Falls.

South Rim

South Rim Drive starts about a half-mile south of Brink of the Upper Falls Road on Grand Loop Road. This drive offers several opportunities to enjoy the Grand Canyon of the Yellowstone. The Upper Falls Viewpoint offers an easy walk to two views of the falls' 109-foot drop. Crystal Falls is also visible across the canyon. Uncle Tom's Trail offers a strenuous walk down more than 300 steps (500

View of the Lower Falls from Artist Point.

feet) into the canyon. At the bottom is a viewing platform where you can feel and see the power of the falls.

At the end of South Rim Drive is Artist Point, which offers a spectacular view of the lower falls and the canyon.

Hayden Valley

About 16 miles south of Canyon Junction, Grand Loop Road runs through the scenic Hayden Valley, site of some of the best wildlife-watching in the park. Bison frequent the area (at times causing traffic jams) as well as moose, elk, coyotes, bears, and trumpeter swans.

Bison in Hayden Valley.

Trails

Point Sublime

Stunning views of the Grand Canyon of the Yellowstone are the reward for hiking the Point Sublime Trail. This relatively moderate trail departs near Artist Point and extends for about a mile and a half along the south rim of the canyon.

View of the canyon from the Point Sublime Trail.

While the views along the way are truly sublime, the trail ends somewhat abruptly at a rough wooden fence without much of a view at all.

Seven Mile Hole

This is one of our favorite hikes. Seven Mile Hole is actually named for its distance below the Lower Falls, not the length of the trail. It's a difficult hike of six miles with 1200 feet of vertical drop that offers a rare opportunity to descend into the canyon all the way down to the

The Seven Mile Hole Trail passes a couple of geysers and hot springs as it descends to the river.

The Yellowstone River at Seven Mile Hole.

river. Along the way, you get views of the 1200-foot Silver Cord Cascade on the opposite rim and pass by a geyser and sulfur thermal area with a couple of hot springs. The trail starts at the Glacier Boulder

Trailhead on the road to Inspiration Point on the north rim of the canyon. There are no water sources along the way, so bring plenty with you for the strenuous 1200-foot climb back out of the canyon.

Mount Washburn

Chittenden Road (about 9½ miles north of Canyon Junction and 8½ miles south of Tower Junction on Grand Loop Road) goes to the top of the mountain but is closed to all but official vehicles after the first mile or so. There's a large parking area for hikers to the left of the gate that serves to close the road. The route up is a steady climb through fields with the distinct possibility of seeing a herd of the bighorn sheep that call the mountain home. At the summit, there's a rather ugly building with an observation deck, restrooms, and drinking water. Alternatively, you can hike to the summit from Dunraven Pass (which is about the same level of difficulty as Chittenden Road) or hike up the steep, lung-busting trail from the Glacial Boulder Trailhead.

A flock of bighorn sheep lives on Mount Washburn and are frequently seen on Chittenden Road.

The view from Mount Washburn.

Fishing Bridge RV Park

Fishing Bridge RV Park

Fishing Bridge RV Park is the only campground in Yellowstone National Park with water, electric (50, 30, and 20 amp), and sewer hookups. It's located in grizzly bear country, and so tents and soft-sided campers (pop-ups) are not allowed for safety reasons. There are also no fire rings or campfires (including portable firepits) allowed. Charcoal and propane grills are allowed, but open flames are not. There is a coin laundry and pay showers (two included per night) located in the camper services building. A Yellowstone General Store offers a selection of camping gear, souvenirs, and groceries as well as a diner/snack bar section that serves breakfast, lunch, and dinner. There's also a dump station near the campground entrance.

The campground has been undergoing major renovations and will be closed until the 2022 season. Upgrades include new and larger sites, a larger parking lot, new dump station and recycling area, and a bigger registration building with a small retail space, more showers, and enlarged laundry facilities. Four comfort stations will also be renovated to bring them up to modern accessibility standards.

The upper loop of the RV park will have 172 renovated and paved sites ranging from 40-foot double-wide lots to sites that can accommodate 95-foot rigs. Many of the remodeled sites will include pull-through drives, and all of the upper loop will have upgraded 50 amp/30 amp and 110-volt electrical services and picnic tables. The remaining sites in the campground will remain double- and single-wide back-in sites accommodating 30-35-foot vehicles. Check www.yellowstonenationalparklodges.com/lodgings/campground/fishing-bridge-rv-park/ for more information.

Campground Details (Prior to Renovations)

Sites	Reservations	Elevation	Accessible Sites	Flush Toilets	Generators (60dB limit)	Big Rig?	Dump Station
310	Yes	7800'	Yes	Yes	8 a.m.–8 p.m.	Up to 40'	Yes

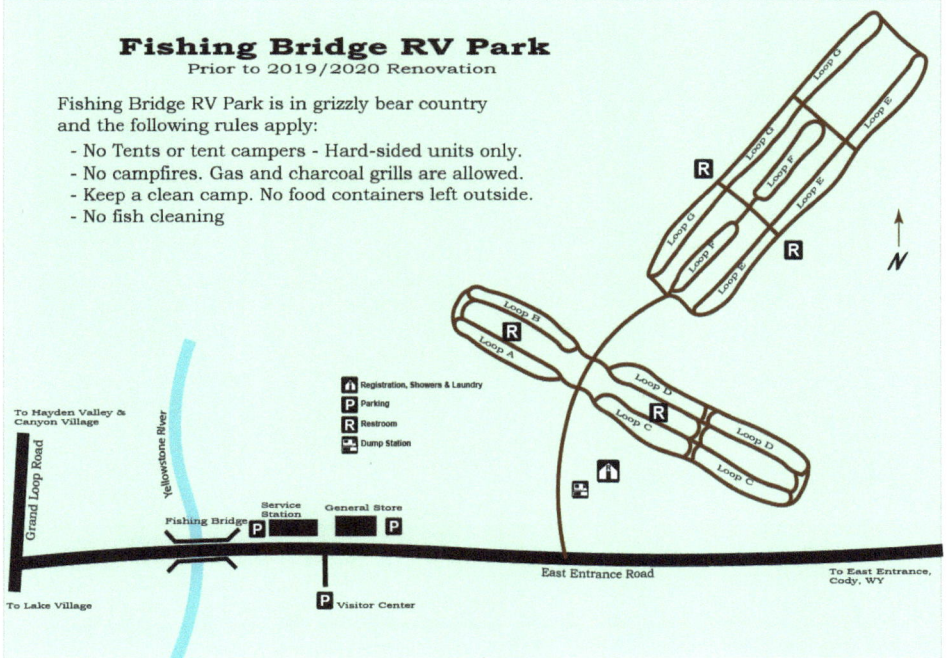

Fishing Bridge RV Park

Fishing Bridge Visitor Center is an excellent example of 1930s "Parkitecture."

Nearby Amenities

Showers	Fishing Bridge RV Park
Laundry	Fishing Bridge RV Park
Restaurant	Fishing Bridge General Store
Groceries	Fishing Bridge
Gas	Fishing Bridge
ATM	Fishing Bridge General Store
Emergency Services	Lake Village

Campground Activities

Fishing Bridge Museum and Visitor Center

A National Historic Landmark, the Fishing Bridge Museum and Visitor Center is located across from the campground on East Entrance Road. It's a great example of the parkitecture of the 1930s and has exhibits on Yellowstone and its wildlife.

Fishing Bridge

The original 1902 Fishing Bridge over the Yellowstone River was replaced by the current structure in 1937. In the early days, it was a popular place for anglers to fish for spawning cutthroat trout. To protect the trout, fishing is no longer allowed from the bridge, but it is an excellent place to watch the spawning fish in June and early July.

Nearby Attractions

Pelican Creek Nature Trail

Just under a mile east of Fishing Bridge is the Pelican Creek Nature Trail. This 1.3-mile loop starts at the west end of the Pelican Creek bridge and goes through old-growth forest to the shore of Yellowstone Lake. A boardwalk trail follows the creek through a marshy area to a beach on the lake. The trail is a great place to view wildflowers. Wildlife in the area include otters, pelicans, ducks, and other birds as well as the occasional grizzly bear.

Mud Volcano

The Mud Volcano was originally a 30-foot-tall volcano-like cone that spewed mud over the trees near it, until a violent eruption apparently blew out the side of it, leaving a crater behind. The area around the volcano includes a variety of thermal features, including Mud Geyser, Mud Caldron, Black Dragon's Caldron and Sour Lake. Across the road from the Mud Volcano is Sulphur Caldron, one of the most acidic features in the park with a pH in the range of battery acid.

The Mud Volcano.

Hayden Valley

Just north of the Mud Volcano, Grand Loop Road returns to the scenic Hayden Valley (see p.49) with its ample wildlife-viewing opportunities.

Hayden Valley is a great place to view bison and other wildlife.

Bridge Bay Campground

Bridge Bay Campground

Bridge Bay Campground is located by Yellowstone Lake about 30 miles from the East Entrance to the park. The campground is

Some sites in Bridge Bay have views of Yellowstone Lake.

noteworthy for its views of both the lake and the Absaroka Mountain Range to the east of the lake. Bridge Bay Marina, the hub for boating with boat rentals and tours on Yellowstone Lake, is next to the campground and has a small store and backcountry office as well.

The campground has over 400 sites in 10 loops, The four lower loops closest to the campground entrance tend to be open fields with few trees, while the six upper loops are more wooded. Some sites have views of Yellowstone Lake. Elk frequent the campground, and you may need to wait for a sleeping elk to get out from under your vehicle before you can leave your site in the morning. Sixteen public restrooms with flush toilets and cold running water are located within the campground. Each restroom also has dishwashing facilities. All campsites have a fire grate, picnic table, and nearby water. There are no showers at Bridge Bay; the nearest ones are located at Grant village.

Sometimes a campsite is just a wide spot in the road, like this one in Bridge Bay.

Campground Details

Sites	Reservations	Elevation	Accessible Sites	Flush Toilets	Generators (60dB limit)	Big Rig?	Dump Station
432	Yes	7800'	Yes	Yes	8 a.m.–8 p.m.	40'+	Yes

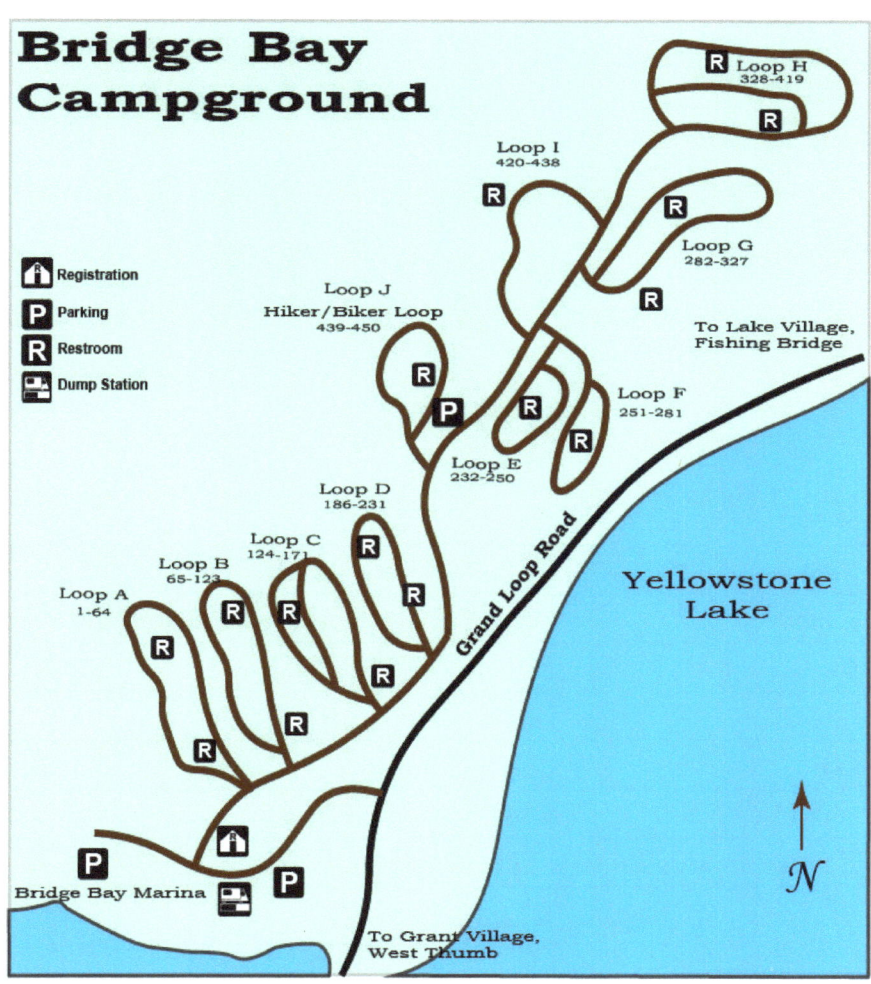

Bridge Bay Campground

Bridge Bay Campground

Yellowstone Lake near Bridge Bay.

Nearby Amenities

Showers	Grant or Fishing Bridge Campground ($)
Laundry	Grant or Fishing Bridge Campground
Restaurant	Lake Village
Groceries	Lake Village
Gas	Fishing Bridge
ATM	Fishing Bridge General Store
Emergency Services	Lake Village

Activities

The activities near Bridge Bay revolve around Yellowstone Lake and the Bridge Bay Marina. Scenic tours of the lake depart from the marina, which also offers powerboat (40hp) rentals, guided fishing charters, slip rentals, and a backcountry shuttle service. Visit www.yellowstonenationalparklodges.com/adventures/water-adventures/ for more information.

Nearby Activities

Natural Bridge Trail

The trail to the Natural Bridge leaves from the campground and follows a former roadway, making it an easy 2½-mile round trip through unburned forest. The paved road is closed to motor vehicles but open to bicycles. There's an interpretive display at the end of the trail that explains how the bridge was formed.

Grant Village Campground

Grant Village Campground

Grant Village is located at the southwest corner of Yellowstone Lake, a few miles from the West Thumb geyser basin. The campground is in a lodgepole pine forest and has a few sites with views of the lake. The campground offers fairly easy access to the lake as well as to the Upper (Old Faithful), Midway, and Black Sand geyser basins.

Grant Campground.

There's an interesting suspension footbridge on the trail from Grant Campground to Grant Village.

Picnic tables are available at every site, as is access to a shared bear-proof food storage box. Pay showers are available at the camper services building at the campground (two included with each night's fee). There are 17 public restrooms in the campground with flush toilets and cold running water. Most of these restroom buildings also have dishwashing facilities.

There are two stores in Grant Village as well as a gas station, restaurant, visitor center, and boat ramp. There are ranger-hosted programs in the evening at the campground amphitheater. There's a trail that goes from the boat launch near the campground over a suspension bridge to the Grant Visitor Center and the Grant Village shops and restaurants.

Campground Details

Sites	Reservations	Elevation	Accessible Sites	Flush Toilets	Generators (60dB limit)	Big Rig?	Dump Station
430	Yes	7800'	Yes	Yes	8 a.m.-8 p.m.	Up to 40'	Yes

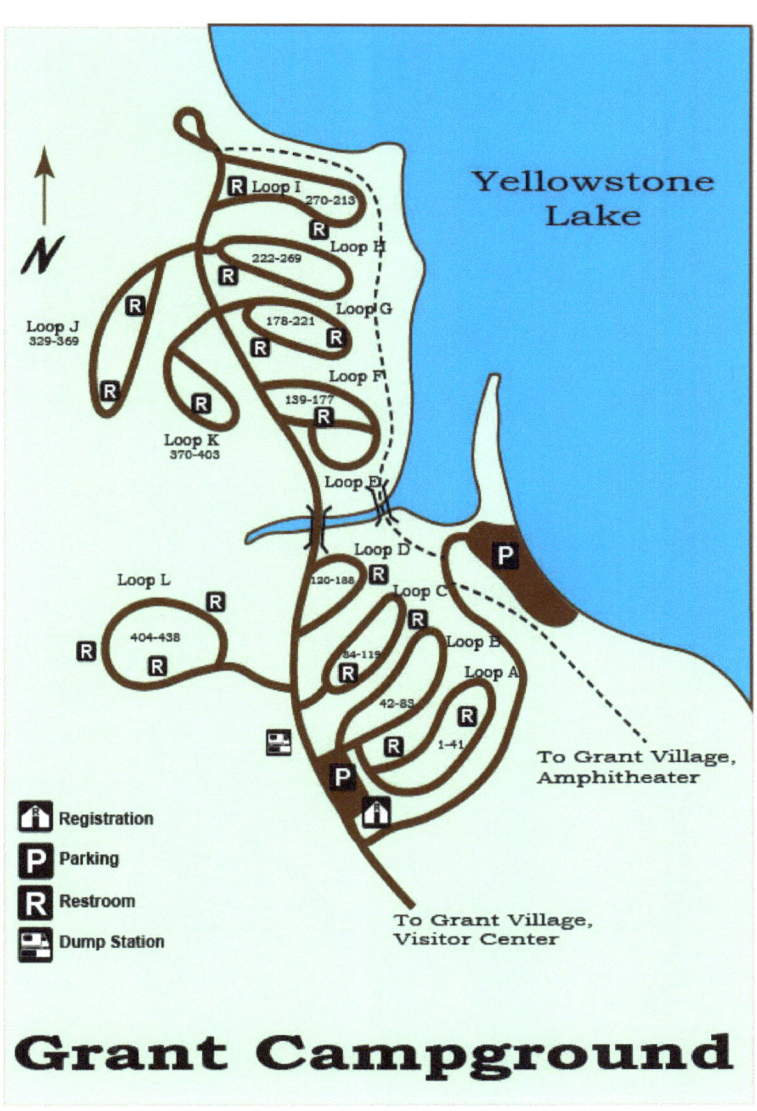

Grant Campground

Grant Village Campground

The evening sky is reflected in Yellowstone Lake near Grant Village.

Nearby Amenities

Showers	Grant Village Campground
Laundry	Grant Village Campground
Restaurant	Grant Village
Groceries	Grant Village General Store
Gas	Grant Village
ATM	Grant Village General Store
Emergency Services	Lake Clinic (Lake Village)

Campground Activities

Ranger programs are hosted each evening from mid-June to September.

Nearby Activities

West Thumb Geyser Basin

Located a couple miles north of Grant Village on Grand Loop Road, West Thumb Geyser Basin is right on Yellowstone Lake. Boardwalks and paved pathways will lead you through the basin's geysers, pools, paint pots, and hot springs, some of which are actually out in the lake. Fishing Cone has been an attraction at the park since the 1870s, when visitors would put on an apron and chef's hat to be photographed with a fishing pole as they cooked their catch on the hook over this geyser. Fishing Cone and its neighbor, Lakeshore Geyser, are both underwater when the lake is high in spring and early summer.

Old Faithful and the Upper Geyser Basin

Grant Campground is the closest campground to the Upper Geyser Basin and the most famous feature in the park: Old Faithful Geyser. Plan to spend at least half a day to see most of what's there. You'll also want to arrive early in the day to ensure you can find a parking space in the peak season (July-August).

It's the most famous, but Old Faithful is only one of hundreds of thermal features in the Upper Geyser Basin.

The Upper Geyser Basin has the world's largest concentration of geysers, and to walk the whole basin is a five-mile hike. Fortunately, because the area is so busy, most of the walking is either on paved trails or boardwalks, so it's easy going.

When you arrive at the basin, check the Old Faithful Visitor Center for eruption times of the major geysers, and pick up a copy of the Old Faithful Trail Guide ($1 donation) to help plan your day. Two additional smaller geyser basins, Black Sand Basin and Biscuit Basin, are adjacent to the main area. Both are accessible either on foot or by car from the Old Faithful area and offer several interesting thermal features.

Old Faithful Visitor Center is the best place to get your bearings before heading out to look at the geyser basin.

A view of the Biscuit, Upper, and Black Sand Geyser Basins.

Midway Geyser Basin

Just a few miles north of Old Faithful on Grand Loop Road is Midway Geyser Basin. The most notable feature here is Grand Prismatic Spring, Yellowstone's largest hot spring. See more information on page 68.

Grand Prismatic Spring is the largest hot spring in Yellowstone and the third-largest in the world.

Lower Geyser Basin (Fountain Paint Pots)

The Lower Geyser Basin, home to Fountain Paint Pots, is just two miles north of Midway Geyser Basin. See page 68 for more information.

Lower Geyser Basin.

Lewis Lake Campground

Lewis Lake Campground

Lewis Lake Campground is about eight miles north of the South Entrance and a short walk from the southeast shore of Lewis Lake. Densely forested by lodgepole pine, each site has a picnic table and firepit with grate. Food storage boxes are available for shared use. A backcountry office is located in the campground. 20 percent of Lewis Lake's campsites are held until 2 weeks prior to arrival, so if you aren't able to book 6 months out it may be your best shot at a site in the park.

Lewis Lake offers backcountry access to Shoshone Lake.

Campground Details

Sites	Reservations	Elevation	Accessible Sites	Flush Toilets	Generators (60dB limit)	Big Rig?	Dump Station
85	Yes	7800'	Yes	No (Vault)	No	25' max	No

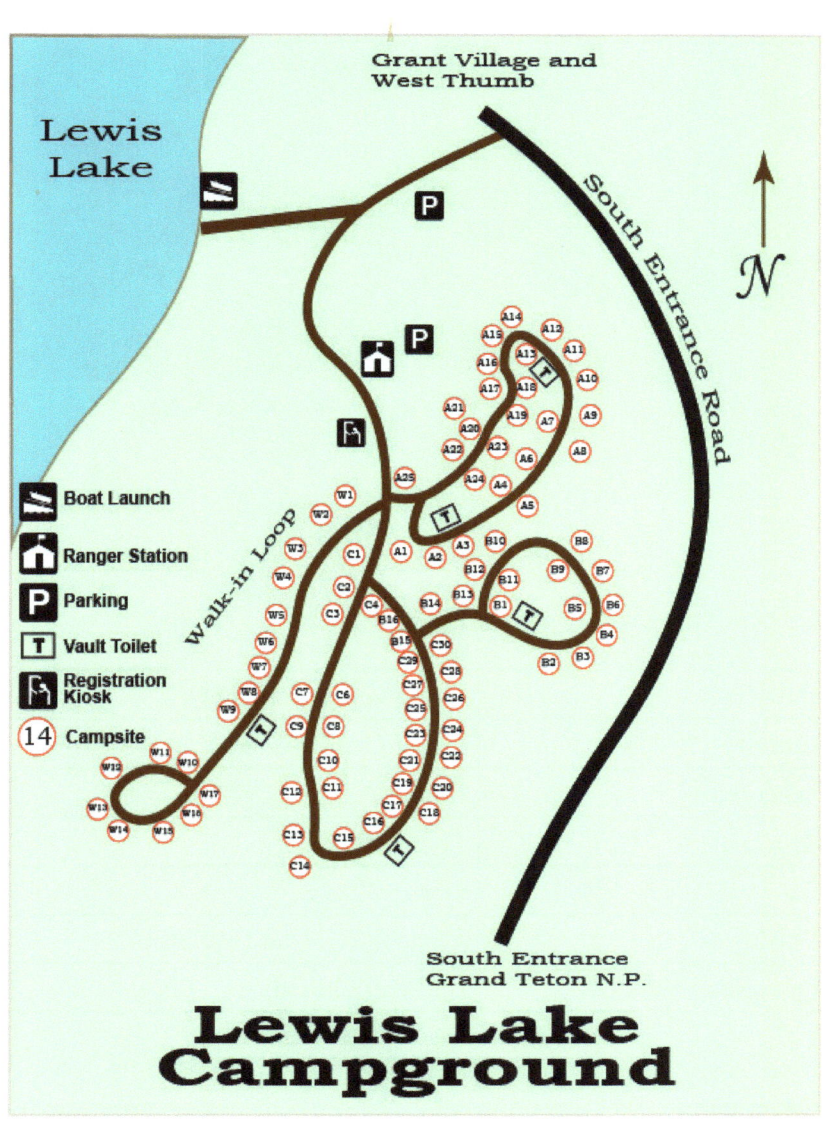

Lewis Lake Campground

Lewis Lake is the jumping-off point for backcountry trips to Shoshone Lake and Geyser Basin.

Nearby Amenities

Showers	Grant Campground ($)
Laundry	Grant Campground
Restaurant	Grant Village
Groceries	Grant Village
Gas	Grant Village
ATM	Grant Village General Store
Emergency Services	Old Faithful Clinic

Campground Activities

Lewis Lake is extremely popular with paddlers, most of whom use it to access Shoshone Lake through the Lewis River Channel. The boat launch is right next to the campground. While it's much smaller than Yellowstone Lake, Lewis Lake can still be whipped up by western winds, so exercise care before attempting an open-water crossing. The Lewis River channel access to Shoshone Lake is at the northwest corner of Lewis Lake. You can paddle up the channel about two miles, after which either the current will be too great to paddle against (spring) or the water will be too shallow (summer). Either way, you'll need to get out and drag your boat. In the spring, when the water is deep and cold, you'll want a wetsuit or drysuit. In later summer, the water is warm and shallow enough that a pair of good water shoes is enough to brave the calf-deep channel.

Shoshone Geyser Basin and its 80 active geysers is found at the northwest corner of Shoshone Lake. An orange marker identifies the landing area to access the basin.

Nearby Attractions

Lewis Lake is the closest campground in Yellowstone to Grand Teton National Park. Grant Village and the West Thumb Geyser Basin are also not too far away from Lewis Lake.

Madison Campground

Madison Campground

Madison Campground is about 14 miles east of West Yellowstone near the junction of West Entrance Road and Grand Loop Road. The Madison River flows past the campground, making it an excellent place for fly-fishing and wildlife-viewing. Along with the fishing and wildlife, the campground is popular for its proximity to some of the most noteworthy thermal features of the park (Old Faithful, Grand Prismatic Spring, etc.) as well as to the town of West Yellowstone.

Each site at the campground has a picnic table, firepit with grate, and shared bear-proof food storage box. Restrooms have flush toilets and running water. Generators are allowed, and a dump station is available. There are 14 public restrooms with flush toilets and cold running water in the campground. Most of these have dishwashing facilities as well.

Madison Campground.

Campground Details

Sites	Reservations	Elevation	Accessible Sites	Flush Toilets	Generators (60dB limit)	Big Rig?	Dump Station
278	Yes	6800'	Yes	Yes	8 a.m.-8 p.m.	Up to 40'	Yes

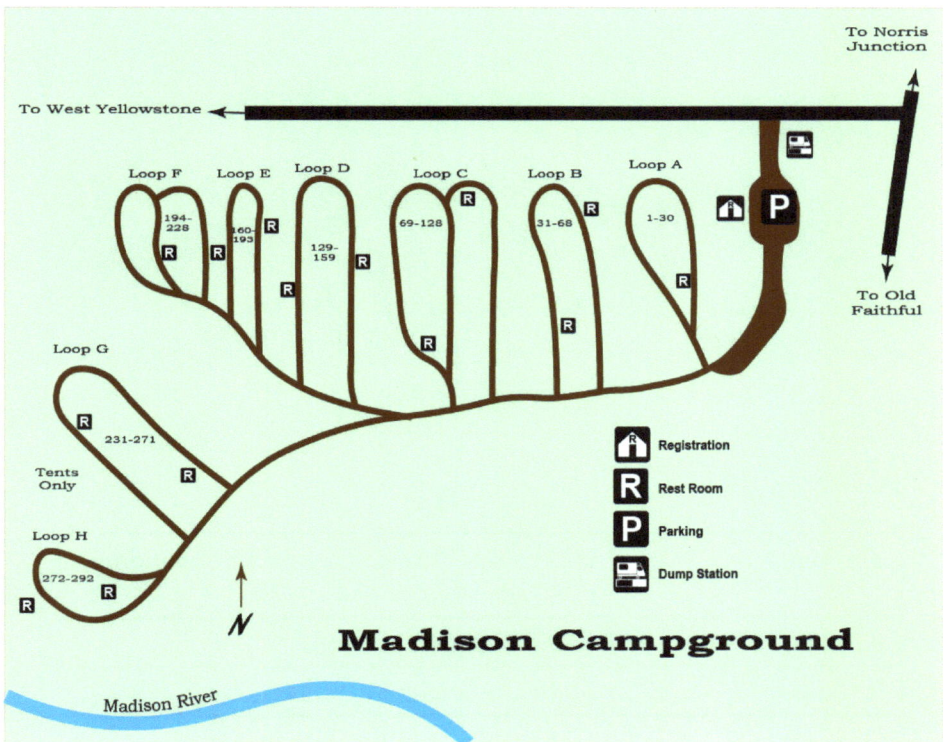

Madison Campground

Madison Campground

The Madison River.

Nearby Amenities

Showers	Old Faithful Inn and Canyon St Laundromat (W. Yellowstone) ($)
Laundry	Snow Lodge (Old Faithful)
Restaurant	Old Faithful and W. Yellowstone
Groceries	Old Faithful and W. Yellowstone
Gas	Old Faithful and W. Yellowstone
ATM	Old Faithful and W. Yellowstone
Emergency Services	Old Faithful Clinic, West Yellowstone Clinic

Nearby Attractions

Firehole Canyon Drive

Just south of Madison Junction on Grand Loop Road is Firehole Canyon Drive, which offers a view of the 40-foot Firehole Falls on the Firehole River.

Lower Geyser Basin—Fountain Paint Pots

The Lower Geyser Basin and Fountain Paint Pots are eight miles south of Madison Junction on Grand Loop Road. You can pick up a trail guide for the half-mile boardwalk loop through the basin at the beginning of the trail. Highlights are the turquoise Silex Spring, blue Celestine Pool, and the bubbling gray and pink Fountain Paint Pots.

Fountain Paint Pots.

Firehole Lake Drive

Firehole Lake Drive is about nine miles south of Madison Junction. Great Fountain Geyser is the highlight of the drive, with its 75-220-foot-high eruptions that last for around an hour. The geyser puts on its show every 10-14 hours. When possible, predicted eruption times may be available at the Old Faithful Visitor Center.

Midway Geyser Basin

Ten miles south of Madison Junction is Midway Geyser Basin, home

Grand Prismatic Spring.

to some of the largest thermal features in the park. The 0.7-mile loop through the basin brings you to the dormant Excelsior Geyser, a captivating turquoise pool. After Excelsior, you will reach Grand Prismatic Spring, the third-largest hot spring in the world and the largest in Yellowstone. The 160 °F turquoise water gives birth to a stunning orange, brown, and gold array with water radiating out in all directions to give it a mirrorlike quality. The smaller (but still large) Turquoise Spring and Indigo Spring round out the display at Midway. For a view of the basin from above, see the Fairy Falls Hike on page 72.

Gibbon Falls.

Gibbon Falls

Gibbon Falls lies on Grand Loop Road between Madison Junction and Norris Junction. There are multiple viewpoints of the nearly 90-foot falls on the interpretive walkway along the road.

Artist's Paint Pots

Artist's Paint Pots are a series of mud pots set into a hillside about four miles south of Norris Junction on Grand Loop Road. The area includes small geysers, pools, and fumaroles with red crusts at the bottom of the hill. A boardwalk and stair trail circles through the features at the base of the hill and up Paint Pot Hill. See page 77 for more information.

Artist's Paint Pots. Early mornings mean fewer people and more mist.

Old Faithful and Upper Geyser Basin

The Upper Geyser Basin and Old Faithful are only about 16 miles south of Madison Junction on Grand Loop Road. See our description of the area on page 60.

Nearby Trails

Fairy Falls

The hike to the 200-foot-tall Fairy Falls is a relatively flat one that goes behind the Grand Prismatic Spring. The trail is accessed from the Fairy Falls Trailhead just south of Midway Geyser Basin on Grand Loop Road. RVs are not allowed in the trailhead parking area, but there is parking along the road for larger vehicles. Get there early to ensure you get a parking spot. Don't be discouraged by the throngs of people headed out on the trail—99 percent of them are going to the Grand Prismatic Spring overlook. This short, steep climb to a breath-taking view of the spring is worth the effort, but we'd recommend taking it on the way back because the steam above the spring (which can obscure the view) dissipates later in the day. After enjoying the falls, be sure to continue on another half-mile (across the stream) to see the Spray and Imperial Geysers.

Fairy Falls is 200 feet tall.

After visiting Fairy Falls, don't miss Imperial Geyser, just another half-mile or so down the trail.

Mystic Falls

Mystic Falls is a pretty 70-foot cascading waterfall that's a relatively easy hike from behind Biscuit Basin. You can either hike out and back, or make a loop of it (and add a more difficult vertical climb) by following the trail past the falls in a lollipop loop. Taking the loop will give you the opportunity to visit the Upper Geyser Basin overlook for a panoramic view of the Biscuit, Black Sand, and Upper Geyser basins.

Mystic Falls.

Norris Campground

Norris Campground

A short (one mile) walk to the Norris Geyser Basin and its central location within the park make Norris Campground an excellent choice. In the peak season, the sites can fill up by 9:00 a.m., so we recommend getting there early to claim a spot. Elk, bears, and bison are frequently seen in the meadow near the lower loop (loop A) and will sometimes wander through the campground.

A lone bison in the field by the Gibbon River at Norris Campground.

Norris has 100 sites located on a hillside near the Gibbon River and Solfatara Creek. Sites at Norris have bear-proof food storage boxes, picnic tables, and fire grates. Firewood and ice are available for purchase

The Norris Campground Office.

Norris campground.

(check at the office for times). The campground is open from late May through late September. Reservations may be made up to six months in advance at www.recreation.gov/.

Campground Details

Sites	Reservations	Elevation	Accessible Sites	Flush Toilets	Generators (60dB limit)	Big Rig?	Dump Station
112	Yes	7500′	Yes	Yes	8 a.m.-8 p.m.	2 @50′ 5 @30′	No

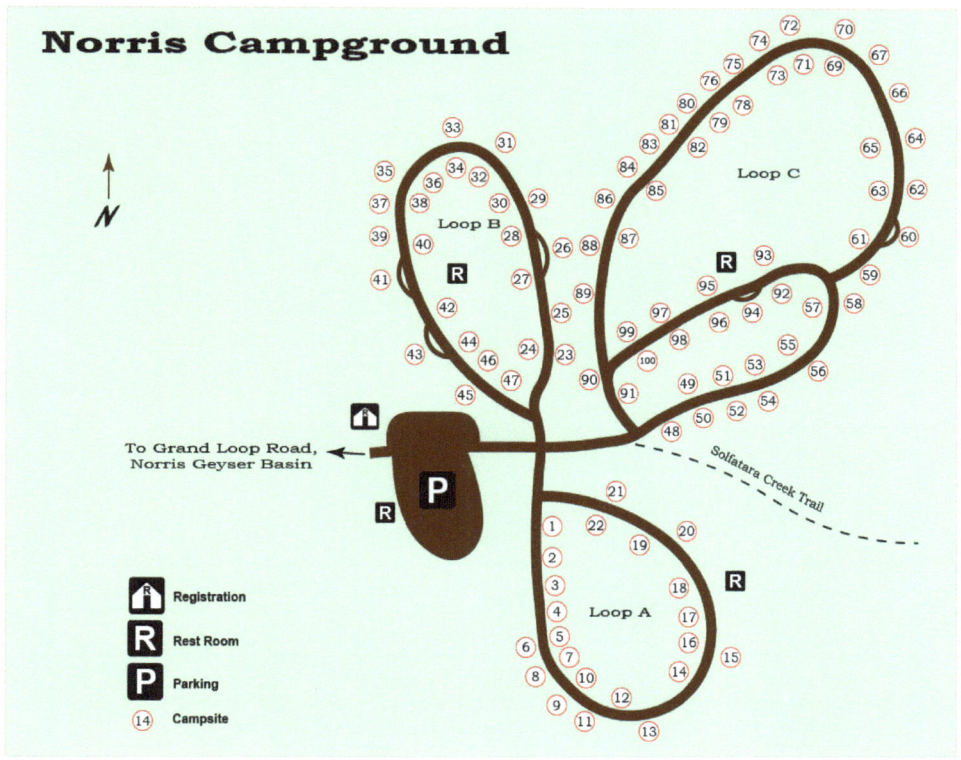

Norris Campground

Porcelain Basin, a part of the Norris Geyser Basin got its name due to its predominately white color.

Nearby Amenities

Showers	Canyon Campground ($)
Laundry	Canyon Campground
Restaurant	Canyon Village
Groceries	Canyon Village
Gas	Canyon Junction
ATM	Canyon Village
Emergency Services	West Yellowstone

Nearby Attractions

Evening Campfire

Norris Campground has a nightly campfire program from June through early September at the Norris Campground campfire circle.

Norris Geyser Basin

Actually comprising two areas—Porcelain Basin and Back Basin—Norris Geyser Basin is the park's hottest thermal area and is a mere one-mile, relatively flat walk from the campground. To reach the geyser basin from the campground, cross Grand Loop Road at the campground entrance and go south (left). The trail will be on your right just after you cross the Gibbon River. When you reach the geyser basin, Porcelain Basin will be on your right. You can either go to the right and loop through that basin or stay to the left and go up the hill to the historic Norris Geyser Basin Museum, where you can pick up a trail guide. You can get a nice overview of the Porcelain basin on the way up to the museum.

Porcelain Basin.

Crackling Lake in Porcelain Basin.

Norris Basin is named for the second superintendent of Yellowstone National Park, Philetus W. Norris, who in addition to leading the construction of some of the first roads in the park also led geographical explorations and was instrumental in developing knowledge of the park's thermal features. As you walk through the basin on the boardwalk, you will see a number of features, including Whale's Mouth and Crackling Lake; the Lodge, Constant, Whirlagig, and Pinwheel Geysers; and Porcelain Springs. Take time to enjoy the wide variety of colors, smells, and sounds before you head up the hill and back to the museum.

Steamboat Geyser, the world's largest, is in Back Basin. Its major eruptions are infrequent, but can reach over 300 feet in height.

Back Basin is on the south side of the museum; its thermal features are more spread out among the forest than those of Porcelain Basin. The world's tallest geyser, Steamboat Geyser, is located here. Its major eruptions can reach over 300 feet in height, but those can be months or years apart. More frequently, it sends water 10-40 feet into the air. Enjoy the variety of other thermal features, including Emerald and Cistern Springs and the Puff 'n Stuff, Porkchop, Pearl, Vixen, and Minute Geysers.

Museum of the National Park Ranger

Located on the entrance road to the campground, the Museum of the National Park Ranger presents an interesting opportunity to learn about the people who take care of and protect our national parks. Originally an outpost for soldiers monitoring the Norris Geyser Basin, the building on the site was erected in 1897 as a replacement for the structure built by the Army in 1886 that was destroyed by fire. The site was completely rebuilt in 1991. Inside the museum, you'll find displays depicting the development of the National Park Service and the park ranger profession and can watch a 25-minute video that tells the story of how the Service developed.

The Museum of the National Park Ranger is in a former ranger station.

Artist's Paint Pots

About 3.7 miles south of Norris Junction lies Artist's Paint Pots, named for its gray pots of burbling mud. There's a mile-long trail on boardwalks, gravel, and stairs that loop around the side of Paint Pot Hill. You'll pass fumaroles, geysers and a few pools and streams as you work your way up the hill toward the paint pots at the top. The Paint Pots have less water available to them than the lower features on the hill and therefore their mud is thicker. Later in the summer as things get drier, they will thicken and even dry up completely. See page 69 for more information.

Artist's Paint Pots on an early morning.

Nearby Trails

Solfatara Creek/Ice Lake Creek Trails

The Solfatara Creek Trail starts near the Norris campfire circle and heads north to meet with Grand Loop Road just south of the Beaver Lake picnic area. The Ice Lake Trail goes to the right about a half-mile up the Solfatara Creek Trail.

Solfatara Creek.

Indian Creek Campground

Indian Creek Campground

Around eight miles south of Mammoth Hot Springs on the road to Norris, Indian Creek Campground sits near the base of the Gallatin Mountains and offers breathtaking views of Electric Peak. This is one of the quieter campgrounds in Yellowstone due to its distance from the highway and is a good place to get away from the crowds at some of the other campgrounds. 20 percent of Indian Creek's campsites are held until 2 weeks prior to arrival, so if you aren't able to book 6 months check here for availability.

Campground Details

Sites	Reservations	Elevation	Accessible Sites	Flush Toilets	Generators (60dB limit)	Big Rig?	Dump Station
70	Yes	7500'	Yes	No (vault)	No	10 @35' 30 @30'	No

Nearby Amenities

Showers	Mammoth Hot Springs Hotel ($)
Laundry	Gardiner
Restaurant	Mammoth Village
Groceries	Gardiner
Gas	Mammoth Village
ATM	Mammoth Village
Emergency Services	Mammoth Clinic (Mammoth Village)

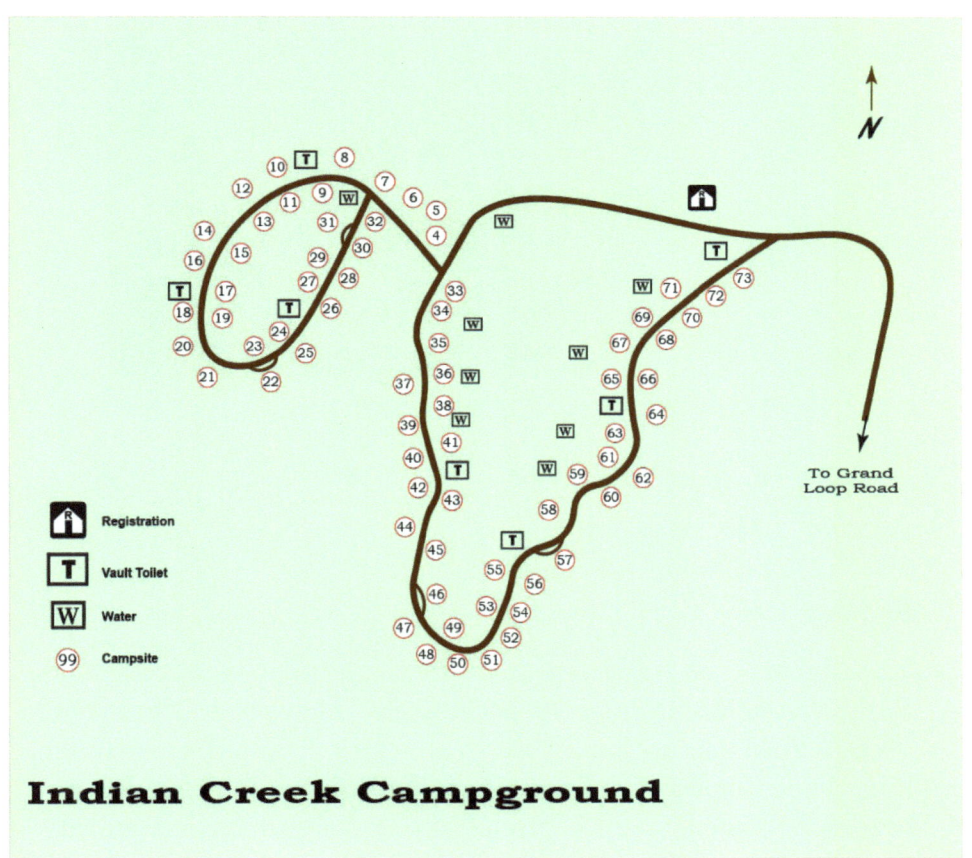

Indian Creek Campground

Indian Creek Campground

Obsidian Creek near Indian Creek Campground.

Nearby Activities

Bighorn Pass

The Bighorn Pass trail leaves from the trailhead on the access road to the campground. It's a 19-mile hike to highway 191 north of West Yellowstone so you'll need to arrange a pickup if you plan to hike the whole way. The route goes through the Gallatin Range bear-management area and groups of 4 or more are recommended. Camping is not allowed within the management area.

Sheepeater Cliff

Sheepeater Cliff, a 500,000-year-old columnar basalt cliff, is about one mile north of the campground on Grand Loop Road. The cliffs were named after a band of Eastern Shoshone known as the Tukuaduka ("sheep eaters") and were formed by one of the basaltic floods of lava in the Yellowstone Caldera.

CAMPGROUNDS OUTSIDE THE PARK

National Forest Service and National Park Campgrounds

The National Forest Service operates quite a few campgrounds near Yellowstone, ranging from rustic open-parking areas with no water or toilets (vault or otherwise) to more developed campgrounds with electric hookups, vault toilets, and water available. Grand Teton National Park is also just south of Yellowstone and has several campgrounds that are within a reasonable driving distance of Yellowstone.

Campground	Location	Rate (RV)	Sites	Longest Site (Total Vehicle)	Water	Toilets	Reservations	Full Hookups	Comments
Baker's Hole Campground	Custer-Gallatin NF (W. Yellowstone)	$ 20	73	75'	Y	V	N	N	33 w/elec. ($28)
Rainbow Point Campground	Custer-Gallatin NF (W. Yellowstone)	$ 20	85	40'	Y	V	Y	N	15 w/elec. ($28)
Lonesomehurst Campground	Custer-Gallatin NF (W. Yellowstone)	$ 20	27	45'	Y	V	Y	N	5 w/elec. ($28)
Cherry Creek Campground	Custer-Gallatin NF (W. Yellowstone)	$ 16	8	*	N	N	N	N	*2 small trailers per site
Spring Creek Campground	Custer-Gallatin NF (W. Yellowstone)	$ 16	6	*	N	V	N	N	*2 RVs per site
Cabin Creek Campground	Custer-Gallatin NF (W. Yellowstone)	$ 20	15	30'	Y	V	N	N	
Beaver Creek Campground	Custer-Gallatin NF (W. Yellowstone)	$ 20	64	30'	Y	V	Y	N	
Cave Falls Campground	Caribou-Targhee N.F. (SW Entrance)	$ 10	23		Y	V	N	N	Grizzly country
Eagle Creek Campground	Custer-Gallatin NF (Gardiner)	$ 15	15	40'	N	V	N	N	
Headwaters Campground	Grand Teton National Park	$103	141	45'	Y	Y	Y	Y	3 miles S of Yellowstone
Lizard Creek Campground	Grand Teton National Park	$ 92	43	30	Y	Y	Y	N	17 walk in tent sites
Colter Bay RV Park	Grand Teton National Park	$112	112	45'	Y	Y	Y	Y	102 Pull-thru sites
Colter Bay Campground	Grand Teton National Park	$ 50	324	45'	Y	Y	Y	N	Dump station available
Timber Camp Campground	Custer-Gallatin NF (Gardiner)	$ -	O*	*	N	N	N	N	*Open parking
Bear Creek Campground	Custer-Gallatin NF (Gardiner)	$ -	O*	*	N	N	N	N	*Open parking
Canyon Campground	Custer-Gallatin NF (Gardiner)	$ 10	15	50'	N	V	N	N	
Soda Butte Campground	Custer-Gallatin NF (Cooke City)	$ 20	27	60'	Y	V	N	N	Hardsided RV only
Colter Campground	Custer-Gallatin NF (Cooke City)	$ 20	18	66'	Y	V	N	N	Hardsided RV only
Threemile Campground	Shoshone NF (East Entrance)	$ 15	21	60'	Y	V	N	N	Hardsided RV only
Eagle Creek Campground	Shoshone NF (East Entrance)	$ 15	20	40'	Y	V	N	N	Hardsided RV only
Newton Creek Campground	Shoshone NF (East Entrance)	$ 15	31	40	Y	V	N	N	Hardsided RV only
Rex Hale Campground	Shoshone NF (East Entrance)	$ 15	30	40'	Y	V	Y	N	8 w/elec ($20)

National Forest and National Park Service Campgrounds Outside Yellowstone National Park

All of the NFS campgrounds near Yellowstone allow generators. None have showers or a dump station.

Gardiner Area (North Entrance)

Eagle Creek Campground, two miles from the North Entrance to Yellowstone

Just two miles northeast of Gardiner on Jardine Road, Eagle Creek Campground has 15 sites and can accommodate RVs up to 40 feet in length; it boasts views of the Electric Mountain range and Mammoth Hot Springs. The nightly fee is $15 and sites are on a first-come, first served basis. Each campsite has a grill and picnic table, but no water is available. There is a horse corral adjacent to two of the campsites. Bear-proof boxes are provided, and safe food storage techniques are required because the campground is in bear country.

Timber Camp Campground, nine miles from the North Entrance to Yellowstone

Located five miles northeast of Gardiner on Jardine Road and then another four miles northeast on Forest Road 493, Timber Camp Campground is a no-reservation, open parking facility. There are no fees and no water, toilets, or other facilities other than a stock corral. This is bear country, and proper storage of food and other attractants is required.

Bear Creek Campground, 9.5 miles from the North Entrance to Yellowstone

Bear Creek Campground is located about a half-mile further down Forest Road 493 than Timber Camp Campground and is another no-fee, open parking camp with a horse corral. There are no water or toilet facilities. This is bear country, and proper storage of food and other attractants is required.

Canyon Campground, 16 miles from the North Entrance to Yellowstone

Canyon Campground is located on US Highway 89, 15 miles north of Gardiner in Yankee Jim Canyon and across the highway from the Yellowstone River. There are 15 sites here that can fit an RV up to 50 feet long. There is no water at the campground, but there are vault toilets. Fire grates and picnic tables are provided. The nightly fee is $10 and reservations are not accepted. This is bear country, and proper storage of food and other attractants is required.

Cooke City–Silver Gate Area (Northeast Entrance)

Colter Campground, seven miles from the Northeast Entrance to Yellowstone

Just east of Cooke City on US 212 (the Beartooth Scenic Highway—see Appendix A on page 90) is the Colter Campground. Due to bear activity, only hard-sided RVs are permitted—no tents or tent trailers allowed. The campground has spectacular views of the surrounding mountains. Camping is first-come, first served, and fees are $20 per night with a $3 charge for extra vehicles. Water is available, and there are picnic tables and fire grates at each site. Bear-proof boxes are provided, and safe food storage techniques are required.

Soda Butte Campground, six miles from the Northeast Entrance to Yellowstone

Soda Butte Campground is a first-come, first-served campground with 27 sites on US Highway 212 (the Beartooth Scenic Highway). Soda Butte is for hard-sided RVs only, no tents or tent campers due to bear activity. Sites have fire rings, picnic tables, and bear-proof storage boxes and can accommodate RVs up to 60 feet long. Vault toilets and water are available. Safe food storage techniques are required. The fee is $20 per night.

Cody/East Entrance

Threemile Campground, three miles from the East Entrance to Yellowstone

The aptly named Threemile Campground lies three miles east of the East Entrance to the park and has 21 sites that can accommodate rigs up to 60 feet long. The campground has some breathtaking views of the Shoshone River; due to grizzly bear activity, it is only open to hard-sided RVs—no tents or tent campers. Bear-proof boxes are provided, and safe food storage techniques are required. Sites are $15 per night and are reservable at www.recreation.gov/. Water (hand-pumped) and accessible vault toilets are available.

Eagle Creek Campground, eight miles from the East Entrance to Yellowstone

Eagle Creek Campground has 20 sites along the Shoshone River and can accommodate rigs up to 40 feet long. Campers can enjoy a footbridge that crosses the river to find an abundance of juniper, fir pine, spruce, wild roses, and wildflowers. Due to grizzly bear activity, Eagle Creek is open to hard-sided RVs only—no tents or tent campers. Bear-proof boxes are provided, and safe food storage techniques are required. Sites are $15 per night. Water (hand-pumped) and accessible vault toilets are available.

Grand Teton National Park Campgrounds Closest to Yellowstone (South Entrance)

All Grand Teton campgrounds are now reservable at www.recreation.gov/.

Headwaters Campground, three miles from Yellowstone

Headwaters Campground and RV Park at Flagg Ranch is located between Yellowstone and Grand Teton National Parks on the John D. Rockefeller Jr. Memorial Parkway (US 89/191/287) a few miles south of Yellowstone's South Entrance. Sites offer water, sewer, and 20/30/50 amp electrical service and can handle rigs up to 45 feet long. Pull-through sites are available, as are laundry facilities, bathrooms, picnic tables, and firepits. Reservations are strongly recommended. The 2022 rate is $103 per night for RV sites and $52 for tent sites; visit recreation.gov/ for more information.

Lizard Creek Campground, 10 miles from Yellowstone

Forty-three RV/tent sites plus 17 walk-in tent sites await you on the shores of Jackson Lake at Lizard Creek Campground. Fishing, canoeing, and kayaking are best in early summer because later in the summer, lake levels drop to expose mud flats rather than rocky beaches. Generators are not allowed in the lower loop, and RVs are limited to no more than 30 feet. Campsites have picnic tables and fire rings, and the campground has restrooms with cold running water. The 2022 rate is $49 for tents and $92 for RVs per night. Visit www.recreation.gov/ for more information.

Colter Bay RV Park, 18 miles from Yellowstone

A five-minute walk from Jackson Lake, the RV park at Colter Bay Village has 103 pull-through and nine back-in sites, all with water, sewer, and electric (20/30/50 amp) hookups. Showers and laundry facilities are available for a fee. Tents and campfires are not permitted, but gas and charcoal grills are allowed. Wi-Fi is available at the nearby restaurants and launderette. The 2022 rate is $112 per night. Visit www.recreation.gov/ for more information.

Colter Bay Campground, 18 miles from Yellowstone

Colter Bay Campground has 335 sites (160 tent spots with pads), 11 group campsites, and 13 electricity-accessible sites. All have picnic tables and fire rings, and bear boxes are available for most tent sites. Restrooms with running water are available, as is a launderette (fee). Individual sites are all first-come, first-served and usually fill between noon and 3:00 p.m. from mid-June through mid-August. The 2022 rate is $50 per night. Visit www.recreation. gov for more information.

West Yellowstone Area (West Entrance)

Baker's Hole, three miles from the West Entrance to Yellowstone

Situated next to the Madison River with views of the mountains in Yellowstone National Park, Baker's Hole Campground has 73 RV and tent sites among lodgepole pines three miles north of West Yellowstone on US Highway 191. Sites are first-come, first-served and 33 of them have electric hookups. None have water or sewer connections, but rigs up to 75 feet long can be accommodated. Vault toilets (some accessible) are available, and there are 12 water spigots in the campground. Sites cost $20 per night, and extra vehicles are $8. Sites with electricity are $28. Firewood is available for purchase. Bear-proof boxes are provided, and safe food storage techniques are required.

Rainbow Point, 10 miles from the West Entrance to Yellowstone

Located on an arm of Hebgen Lake, Rainbow Point Campground has 86 sites, 46 with electric hookups. The 2021 rate was $20 per night, $28 for sites with electricity. To reach the campground, drive 4.6 miles north of West Yellowstone on US 191/287 and turn left at the sign for Rainbow Point. Drive 3.7 miles and turn right on Forest Rt. 6954, a dirt road, for about another two miles. The area is heavily wooded, and all of the sites are a short walk from the lake. There is a boat launch at the campground, and firewood is available for purchase. Water and vault toilets are available, some of which are handicap accessible.

Lonesomehurst, 12 miles from the West Entrance to Yellowstone

Popular with kayakers and canoeists due to its location by Hebgen Lake, Lonesomehurst Campground has 27 sites (some reservable at www.recreation.gov/) in a stand of lodgepole pine. Lonesomehurst is 3.5 miles north off of US 20, 7.2 miles west of its intersection with US 191. The fee for camping is $20 a night ($28 for sites with electricity) and another $8 for an additional vehicle. Many of the sites overlook the South Fork of the lake. Sites have picnic tables and grills, and firewood is available for purchase. Water and vault toilets (some accessible) are available; five of the sites have electricity. This is bear country, and proper storage of food and other attractants is required.

Cherry Creek, 14 miles from the West Entrance to Yellowstone

Located eight miles west on US 20 and then six miles north on Denny Creek Road, Cherry Creek Campground has eight sites by Hebgen Lake available first-come, first-served that cost $16 per night. There are no toilets, and water is not available at the campground. There is no trash service at Cherry Creek—you must pack out your own trash.

Spring Creek Campground, 18 miles from the West Entrance to Yellowstone

Eight miles west of West Yellowstone and 10 miles north on Hebgen Lake Road, this first-come, first-served campground has six sites on Hebgen Lake. There is no fee for camping, and accessible vault toilets are available.

Cabin Creek, 22 miles from the West Entrance to Yellowstone

Cabin Creek Campground offers 15 wooded sites (some reservable at www.recreation.gov/) for $20 per night ($8 for additional vehicle). Sites have picnic tables and grills and can accommodate up to 30-foot-long RVs. Firewood is available for purchase; water is also available. Bear-proof boxes are provided, and safe food storage techniques are required as this campground is in bear country.

Beaver Creek, 24 miles from the West Entrance to Yellowstone

Eight miles north of West Yellowstone on US 191 and then another 16 miles west on US 287 sits Beaver Creek Campground with its 64 sites by Earthquake Lake, which was formed when the Madison River was dammed by an earthquake-induced landslide in 1959. You can visit the Forest Service's Earthquake Lake Visitor Center 3.7 miles west of the campground for a more detailed story of lake's formation. Sites are $20 per night and some are reservable at www.recreation.gov/. Sites are all back-in and the longest are 30 feet. None of the sites have hookups, but vault toilets (some accessible) and water spigots are available. Sites are distributed in three loops throughout a mixture of aspen, Engelmann spruce, and lodgepole pine as well as wildflower fields. Firewood is available for purchase, and bear-proof boxes are provided. Safe food storage techniques are required.

Cave Falls

About 80 miles from West Yellowstone but just outside the Bechler Ranger Station is Cave Falls Campground in the rarely visited southwest corner of the park. The ranger station is inside the park although not accessible to the rest of Yellowstone other than via a 50-mile trip including dirt roads best suited for four-wheel drive vehicles. It is primarily a jumping-off point for backcountry enthusiasts interested in the waterfalls and rivers of this part of the park. The campground sits along the Falls River and most sites offer river views. Cave Falls is about a mile from the campground. Amenities include water and vault toilets; the fee is $10 per night. From Ashton, ID, take State Rt. 47 east 5.3 miles, where you'll see a sign for Yellowstone National Park/Cave Falls. Take a right, go 18.3 miles, and the campground will be on your right.

Private RV Parks

There are a number of private RV parks in Gardiner and West Yellowstone that offer full hookup campsites as well as access to the restaurants, shops and other amenities these towns have to offer. All of them have full hookups, Wi-Fi, and showers.

Campground	Location	Rate	Sites	Longest Site	Toilets	Tents Sites	Full Hookups	Dump Station	Comments
Rocky Mountain Campground	Gardiner	$ 89	71	*	Y	N	Y		* Can accommodate big rigs.
Yellowstone RV Park	Gardiner	$ 89	46	65'	F	Y	Y		Limited # of 50 amp sites
Yellowstone Grizzly RV	West Yellowstone	$110	261	80'	F	N	Y	Y	Near Grizzly Center & Downtown
Fort Jax RV Park	West Yellowstone	*	19		F		Y		*Caters to seasonal guests.
Buffalo Crossing RV Park	West Yellowstone	$ 85	25	70'	F	N	Y	Y	Near downtown.
Yellowstone KOA West Gate	West Yellowstone	$113	300+	77'	F	Y	Y	Y	Tour shuttle & cabins available.
Yellowstone KOA Mountainside	West Yellowstone	$ 95	100	105'	F	Y	Y		Tour shuttle & cabins available.
Wagon Wheel RV Campground	West Yellowstone	$ 79	32	40'	F		Y	Y	In town.
Pony Express RV Park	West Yellowstone	$ 55	16	35'	F	N	Y	N	Shares property with motel.

Private Campgrounds Outside Yellowstone National Park

Gardiner

Rocky Mountain Campground

A quarter mile from the North Entrance to Yellowstone National Park in Gardiner is Rocky Mountain RV Park and Cabins, offering full-hookup sites with Wi-Fi. Showers are available, and restaurants and groceries are within walking distance.
www.rockymountainrvpark.com
14 Jardine Road, Gardiner, Montana 59030
(406) 848-7251

Yellowstone RV Park

Located along the Yellowstone River just outside Gardiner, Yellowstone RV Park has 46 sites overlooking the river. One mile from the North Entrance, it offers some pull-through sites and features amenities including Wi-Fi, cable TV, laundry, and showers.
www.rvparkyellowstone.com
121 Hwy. 89 South, Gardiner, Montana 59030
(406) 848- 7496

West Yellowstone

Yellowstone Grizzly RV Park

Located a few blocks from downtown shopping and restaurants and bordering the Custer-Gallatin National Forest, Grizzly RV Park has 261 campsites including pull-through sites up to 80 feet long, full hook-ups with 30-50 amp service, water, sewer, cable TV, and Wi-Fi. Tents are not allowed. There are six bathhouses in the park and four laundry rooms. Sites have gravel pads, and although not especially wide, they will accommodate slide-outs, and due to well-placed trees and meticulous grooming of the grounds, feel quite private. No open wood fires are allowed, but propane or charcoal fires are OK. www.grizzlyrv.com
210 S. Electric St., West Yellowstone, MT (406) 646-4466

The Union Pacific Railroad Station is now a museum in West Yellowstone.

Wagon Wheel RV and Cabins

Wagon Wheel RV offers 32 sites just a couple of blocks from the West Entrance to Yellowstone Park as well as from the shops and restaurants in the town of West Yellowstone. Pull-through and back-in sites are available to accommodate rigs up to 40 feet in length; most sites have full hookups (water, electric, sewer). Wi-Fi is available for free in public areas and DirecTV is also available. www.yellowstonervcabin.com
408 Gibbon Ave, West Yellowstone, MT 59758 (406) 646-7872

Sites in Grizzly RV Park are not huge but well maintained.

Fort Jax RV Park

Full hookup sites catering to long-term and seasonal guests.
www.visitmt.com/listings/general/private-campground/fort-jax-
rv-park.html
615 Madison Ave, West Yellowstone, MT 59758
(406) 646-7729

Pony Express RV Park

Across the street from the park and just a few blocks from the
West Entrance to Yellowstone, Pony Express RV Park is also right
in town and within walking distance of shopping and restaurants.
The camp offers amenities including a laundry, free showers, and
complimentary Wi-Fi and cable TV.
www.brandiniron.com/pony-express-rv-resort
3 Firehole Ave, West Yellowstone, MT 59758
(800) 217-4613

Buffalo Crossing RV Park

Buffalo Crossing RV Park is the newest RV park and the closest
to the West Entrance to Yellowstone. It's also within walking
distance of downtown West Yellowstone. Amenities at the park
include a large retail store, giant-screen theater, Wi-Fi, laundry
rooms, and restrooms with showers. The camp has pull-through
and back-in sites that can accommodate rigs up to 70 feet long;
sites include 20/30/50 amp electrical service, water and sewer.
Tents are not allowed.
www.buffalocrossingrvpark.com
101 B South Canyon St, West Yellowstone, MT 59758
(406) 646-4300

Yellowstone KOA West Gate

Six miles from the West Entrance to Yellowstone Park on US
Highway 20 is the Yellowstone KOA West Gate. This large,

well-developed campground has a wide range of amenities including a pool, hot tub/sauna, snack bar, mini golf, bike rentals, a tour shuttle, and a pavilion. Campfires are allowed, and each site has a fire ring and picnic table. Between June 1 and Labor Day, breakfast and dinner are served every day. Sites can accommodate rigs up to 90 feet long and are available in both pull-through and back-in styles with 30/50 amp service, water, and electric hookups. Tents are allowed and cabins are also available.

www.koa.com

3305 Targhee Pass Highway, West Yellowstone, MT 59758

(406) 646-7606

Yellowstone KOA/Mountainside

A mile and a half west of the West Gate KOA on US 20 is another KOA park, the Yellowstone Mountainside KOA. This campground can handle units up to 105 feet long and boasts both pull-through and back-in sites with full hookups. Tents are allowed. Camping cabins are available as well as a Super 8 motel sharing the property for any non-camping friends. Amenities include a laundry, snack bar, fishing, cable TV, and a tour shuttle. Campfires are allowed; each site has a fire ring and picnic table.

www.koa.com

3305 Targhee Pass Highway, West Yellowstone, MT 59758

(406) 646-7662

APPENDIX A
THE BEARTOOTH HIGHWAY:
AN UNFORGETTABLE EXIT

US Highway 212 between Red Lodge and Cooke City, Montana, winds its way over the 11,000′ Beartooth Pass through over 1 million acres of wilderness in the Custer-Gallatin (Montana) and Shoshone (Wyoming) National Forests as the Beartooth Highway. Charles Kuralt, in his television show *On the Road,* called it "the most beautiful drive in America," and we're not going to argue the point. Traversing lush forests and alpine tundra, the drive offers magnificent views and a number of places to camp along the way. While you can certainly

View from the Rock Creek Vista on the Beartooth Highway.

enter the park via the Beartooth Highway, we prefer to save it for the drive out, using Yellowstone's 6-7000′ elevations as an opportunity to acclimate before attempting the 10-11,000′ elevations of the Beartooth. It's also a nice way to wrap up the trip by unwinding in the quiet of the mountains after dealing with the park's crowds.

It's a challenging drive with a number of switchbacks, long climbs, and descents as the road goes from 7600′ elevation in Cooke City over the nearly 11,000′ Beartooth Pass and back down to 5500′ in Red Lodge, but the roads are well maintained and any vehicle in reasonably good condition should not have a problem. Be sure to downshift on long descents to

Both Montana and Wyoming have upgraded the highway in recent years.

avoid overheating your brakes. Extremely long vehicle combinations (over 40′) may have issues on some of the tighter curves.

There are 13 National Forest Service Campgrounds along the highway with over 200 sites. Most of

Passenger's view of the Beartooth Highway.

them are first-come, first-served, but a few do take reservations. Check www.recreation.gov/ for more information. These campgrounds offer some beautiful sites in a spectacularly quiet environment—the perfect opportunity to recuperate after the hustle and bustle of life in the park.

Forest Service campsites in the Beartooth offer more quiet and privacy than those in Yellowstone.

Island Lake on the Beartooth Highway.

Campground	Location	Rate (2019)	Sites	Longest Site (Total Vehicle)	Water	Toilets	Reservations	Dump Station	Comments
National Forest Campgrounds on the Beartooth Highway									
Gallatin NF Campgrounds (Montana)									
Soda Butte Campground	1 mi east of Cooke City	$ 20	27	48'	Y	V	N	N	Hard-sided RV's only.
Colter Campground	2 mi east of Cooke City	$ 20	18	48'	Y	V	N	N	Hard-sided RV's only.
Shoshone NF Campgrounds (Wyoming)									
Fox Creek Campground	7 mi east of Cooke City	$ 20	33	32'	Y	V	N	N	Closed for 2019.
Crazy Creek Campground	11 mi east of Cooke City	$ 10	16	28'	N	V	N	N	Recently upgraded.
Beartooth Lake Campground	31 mi south of Red Lodge	$ 15	20	32'	Y	V	N	N	Store nearby.
Island Lake Campground	29 mi south of Red Lodge	$ 15	20	32'	Y	V	N	N	Store nearby.
Custer NF Campgrounds (Montana)									
M-K Campground	12 mi south of Red Lodge	Free	10	20'	N	V	N	N	Open year round.
Greenough Lake Campground	12 mi south of Red Lodge	$ 17	18	45'	Y	V	Y	N	Walking distance to lake.
Limber Pine Campground	12 mi south of Red Lodge	$ 18	13	45'	Y	V	Y	N	On Rock Creek.
Parkside Campground	12 mi south of Red Lodge	$ 18	28	40'	Y	V	Y	N	On Rock Creek.
Rattin Campground	8 mi south of Red Lodge	$ 17	6	20'	Y	V	Y	N	On Rock Creek.
Sheridan Campground	6 mi south of Red Lodge	$ 17	9	30'	Y	V	Y	N	On Rock Creek.

APPENDIX B
YELLOWSTONE LODGING

If you'd like a break from camping, there are nine lodges where you can get either a cabin or a hotel style room. All of them are reservable through http://www.yellowstonenationalparklodges. com/. Reservations book far in advance so get them early.

Yellowstone Lodging	
Canyon Lodge & Cabins	Over 400 rooms in five hotel-style lodges plus over a hundred more rustic cabins
Grant Village Lodge	300 hotel-style rooms in six two-story lodges
Lake Hotel & Cabins	Large lodge with both hotel-style and cabin accommodations
Lake Lodge Cabins	186 cabins
Mammoth Hot Springs Hotel & Cabins	Large lodge with both hotel-style and cabin accommodations
Old Faithful Inn	Iconic rustic lodge with hotel-style accommodations
Old Faithful Snow Lodge	Large Lodge with both hotel-style rooms and cabins
Roosevelt Lodge	Iconic lodge with cabin accommodations

APPENDIX C
DINING IN YELLOWSTONE

There are over 20 restaurants in Yellowstone are listed in the table below. They range from simple grab & go to full-service sit-down establishments with creative cuisine featuring locally sourced food. Check https://www.yellowstonenationalparklodges.com/dining/ for more information.

Yellowstone Restaurants	
Canyon Village	
Canyon Lodge Eatery	Cafeteria style Asian bowls & comfort food.
Falls Café	Grab & go flatbreads, sandwiches & snacks.
Ice Creamery	As the name indicates, ice cream.
M66 Grill	Full-service dining.
Canyon General Store	50's style soda fountain – burgers, breakfast.
Grant Village	
Grant Village Lodge Dining Room	Full-service restaurant.

Yellowstone Restaurants	
Lake House at Grant*	Full-service restaurant
Grant Village General Store	Grill & ice cream counter.
Lake Village	
Lake Hotel Dining Room*	Full-service restaurant.
Lake Lodge Cafeteria	Cafeteria open for lunch & dinner.
Lake General Store	Concession & ice cream counter.
Fishing Bridge	
Fishing Bridge General Store	Grill & ice cream counter.
Mammoth Hot Springs	
Mammoth Hotel Dining Room	Sit-down breakfast, lunch & dinner
Terrace Grill	Quick service burgers, sandwiches
Map Room Bar	Espresso, coffee, tea, full bar
Old Faithful	
Old Faithful Inn Dining Room*	Full-service restaurant.
Bear Paw Deli	Quick service deli-style.
Obsidian Dining Room (Snow Lodge)*	Full-service restaurant.
Geyser Grill	Quick service burgers, sandwiches.
Old Faithful Lodge Cafeteria	Cafeteria-style lunch & dinner.
Old Faithful Lodge Bake Shop	Muffins, bagels, sandwiches & ice cream.
Old Faithful General Stores	Concession, grill & ice cream counter.
Tower/Roosevelt	
Roosevelt Lodge Dining Room	Full-service restaurant.
Old West Dinner Cookout	Outdoor western barbecue.

*Reservations required for dinner.

APPENDIX D
OUR CAMPING EQUIPMENT

Over the years, we've camped in everything from tents to popup campers, travel trailers, and class C and class A motorhomes. All have been fun and have their own compromises between cost, space, and drivability according to our needs at the time. These days we prefer camping in national parks, state parks, and National Forest Service campgrounds, where things are a little quieter, more rustic, and a bit more private than most commercial RV parks. In these campgrounds, hookups are less likely and longer spaces are harder to find, which led us to choose a relatively small motorhome as our primary camper.

Our current camper is a 25-foot Forester class C motorhome built on the Mercedes Sprinter diesel chassis. For us, it's perfect: enough room not to be claustrophobic, yet small enough to get 14 miles to the gallon on average, and not much more difficult to drive than a large SUV. It's also small enough to fit on almost any campsite wherever we go and isn't too hard to park when we use it like a car to drive to an attraction. That's especially important in places like Yellowstone, where many campsites are less than 30 feet long.

It has its own bathroom, and with about 35 gallons each of water/wastewater/black water capacity, we can get through three or so days without too much trouble before having to empty the tanks. Navy showers and minimal use of water for dishes help extend our stays. We have added 200 watts of solar panels on the roof that charge the batteries fairly quickly on a sunny day. We do have a built-in generator, which we try to use as little as possible (even when allowed by campground rules) to charge up our lithium batteries. We upgraded to lithium both because lithium batteries are able to charge more quickly and discharge to a deeper level without damage and because they weigh significantly less than the equivalent usable capacity of traditional lead-acid batteries.

Nothing beats a campfire in the mountains …

www.ingramcontent.com/pod-product-compliance
Lightning Source LLC
Chambersburg PA
CBHW040854120626
46551CB00001B/19